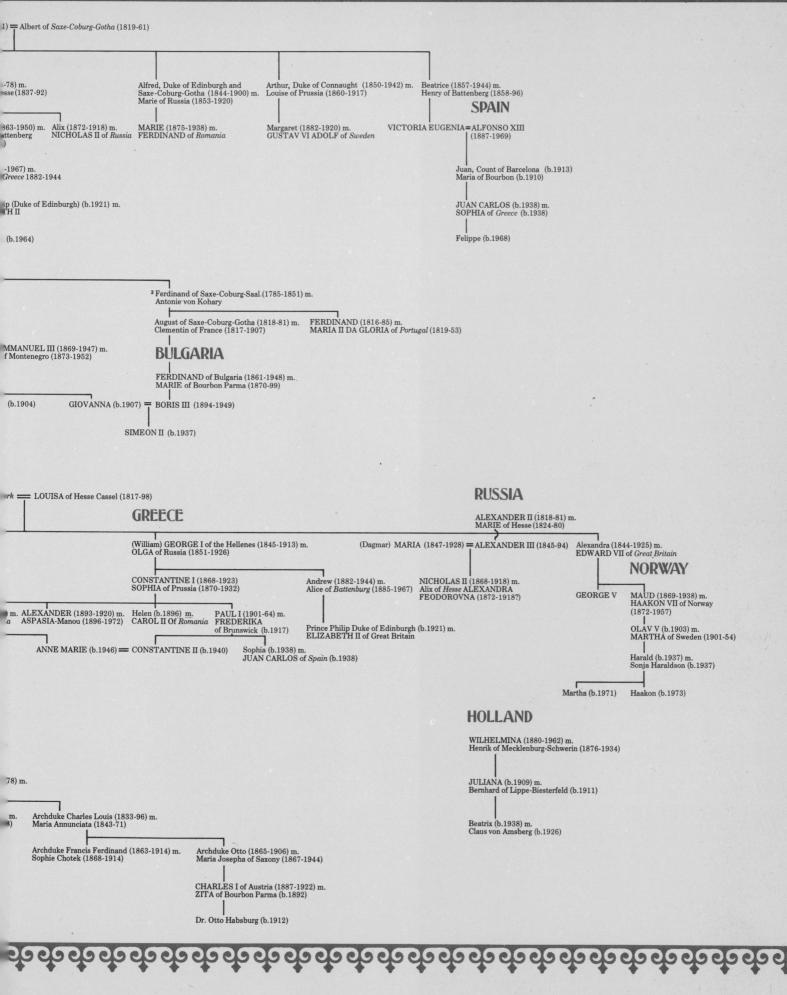

1) = Albert of *Saxe-Coburg-Gotha* (1819-61)

-78) m.
sse (1837-92)

Alfred, Duke of Edinburgh and
Saxe-Coburg-Gotha (1844-1900) m.
Marie of Russia (1853-1920)

Arthur, Duke of Connaught (1850-1942) m.
Louise of Prussia (1860-1917)

Beatrice (1857-1944) m.
Henry of Battenberg (1858-96)

SPAIN

863-1950) m.
attenberg

Alix (1872-1918) m.
NICHOLAS II of *Russia*

MARIE (1875-1938) m.
FERDINAND of *Romania*

Margaret (1882-1920) m.
GUSTAV VI ADOLF of *Sweden*

VICTORIA EUGENIA = ALFONSO XIII
(1887-1969)

-1967) m.
Greece 1882-1944

Juan, Count of Barcelona (b.1913)
Maria of Bourbon (b.1910)

ip (Duke of Edinburgh) (b.1921) m.
'H II

JUAN CARLOS (b.1938) m.
SOPHIA of *Greece* (b.1938)

(b.1964)

Felipe (b.1968)

---

² Ferdinand of Saxe-Coburg-Saal.(1785-1851) m.
Antonie von Kohary

August of Saxe-Coburg-Gotha (1818-81) m.
Clementin of France (1817-1907)

FERDINAND (1816-85) m.
MARIA II DA GLORIA of *Portugal* (1819-53)

MMANUEL III (1869-1947) m.
f Montenegro (1873-1952)

BULGARIA

FERDINAND of Bulgaria (1861-1948) m.
MARIE of Bourbon Parma (1870-99)

(b.1904)

GIOVANNA (b.1907) = BORIS III (1894-1949)

SIMEON II (b.1937)

---

rk = LOUISA of Hesse Cassel (1817-98)

RUSSIA

GREECE

ALEXANDER II (1818-81) m.
MARIE of Hesse (1824-80)

(William) GEORGE I of the Hellenes (1845-1913) m.
OLGA of Russia (1851-1926)

(Dagmar) MARIA (1847-1928) = ALEXANDER III (1845-94)

Alexandra (1844-1925) m.
EDWARD VII of *Great Britain*

NORWAY

CONSTANTINE I (1868-1923)
SOPHIA of Prussia (1870-1932)

Andrew (1882-1944) m.
Alice of *Battenburg* (1885-1967)

NICHOLAS II (1868-1918) m.
Alix of *Hesse* ALEXANDRA
FEODOROVNA (1872-1918?)

GEORGE V

MAUD (1869-1938) m.
HAAKON VII of Norway
(1872-1957)

m. ALEXANDER (1893-1920) m.
a ASPASIA-Manou (1896-1972)

Helen (b.1896) m.
CAROL II Of *Romania*

PAUL I (1901-64) m.
FREDERIKA
of Brunswick (b.1917)

Prince Philip Duke of Edinburgh (b.1921) m.
ELIZABETH II of Great Britain

OLAV V (b.1903) m.
MARTHA of Sweden (1901-54)

ANNE MARIE (b.1946) = CONSTANTINE II (b.1940)

Sophia (b.1938) m.
JUAN CARLOS of *Spain* (b.1938)

Harald (b.1937) m.
Sonja Haraldson (b.1937)

Martha (b.1971)

Haakon (b.1973)

HOLLAND

WILHELMINA (1880-1962) m.
Henrik of Mecklenburg-Schwerin (1876-1934)

78) m.

JULIANA (b.1909) m.
Bernhard of Lippe-Biesterfeld (b.1911)

m.
)

Archduke Charles Louis (1833-96) m.
Maria Annunciata (1843-71)

Beatrix (b.1938) m.
Claus von Amsberg (b.1926)

Archduke Francis Ferdinand (1863-1914) m.
Sophie Chotek (1868-1914)

Archduke Otto (1865-1906) m.
Maria Josepha of Saxony (1867-1944)

CHARLES I of Austria (1887-1922) m.
ZITA of Bourbon Parma (b.1892)

Dr. Otto Habsburg (b.1912)

Terry -

Perhaps this will help straighten them all out!

Christmas, 1979.

Sharon

The Royal Families of Europe

The Royal

Families of Europe

Geoffrey Hindley

CHARTWELL
BOOKS INC.

Published by Chartwell Books Inc.
A Division of Book Sales Inc.
110 Enterprise Avenue
Secaucus, New Jersey 07094
© 1979 Lyric Books Limited
Depósito legal   TO - 556 - 79
ISBN 0 7111 0005 5
Impreso en Artes Gráficas Toledo
Printed in Spain

Contents

Foreword

The actual powers of modern kings and queens are often so slight that their office appears to some an out of date remnant from bygone times. Nevertheless Japan, the world's most successful contemporary economy is ruled by an emperor who formally renounced his divine status barely thirty years back, while more than half the member states of the European Economic Community are ruled by monarchs. Indeed such is the mutual esteem of the royal club that when, in Spring 1979, Queen Elizabeth II toured the Arab states she was welcomed with the respect due to her rank as a reigning sovereign and, though a woman, treated as an equal by Islamic rulers, whose religion and societies confine women to a subordinate role. Thus, for a moment, did the world's oldest political institution serve as envoy for feminism, the most recent political lobby.

Such adaptability to changes in the world should come as no surprise. The ancient monarchies of Europe which survive today have done so precisely because they have proved able to transform themselves to suit changing circumstances. In Spain, the institution of monarchy has even been restored after an interregnum of four decades as the one symbol of political unity acceptable to a divided nation.

Elsewhere in Europe the birth of new nations or the rebirth of old ones, was sanctified by coronations. Between 1830 and 1930, Belgium, Greece, Italy, Norway, Romania, Bulgaria and Yugoslavia, were all inaugurated into the ranks of the world's sovereign states by newly established royal houses, and even modern Germany first achieved united statehood in 1871 under the sovereignty of a newly created empire. In other words, for 150 years after the French Revolution seemed to have shattered the fabric of royal Europe, statesmen were still finding useful jobs for monarchy to do.

In 1901, the year of Queen Victoria's death, all of Europe outside France, Switzerland and San Marino was under the sway of sovereign princes. Today, the old continent can still boast ten reigning sovereigns. But they, and the descendants of many royal houses now exiled from power still form an elite club to whose members still clings the aura of past majesty.

It is this story with its victories and defeats, intrigues and romance, that my book sets out to relate, in a manner which is, I trust, as entertaining as it is informative.

Geoffrey Hindley

Half-title page: *King of Sweden (Camera Press)*
Title pages: *Wilhelm I in the Franco-Prussian war (Mary Evans Picture Library)*
Contents pages: *Escorial, Madrid (Zefa Picture Library)*
Left: *Castle Herrenchiemsee (Zefa Picture Library)*

THE ROYAL FAMILY OF ENGLAND
1863.

Victorian Prelude

'Seated upon St Edward's chair, the Dalmatic robe was clasped about me by the Lord Great Chamberlain. Then followed all the various things; and last the Crown being placed on my head – which was, I must own, a most beautiful, impressive moment; *all* the Peers and Peeresses put on their coronets at the same instant . . . The shouts, which were very great, the drums, the trumpets, the firing of the guns, all at the same instant, rendered the spectacle most imposing. . . . I shall always remember this day as the *Proudest* of my life! I came home at a little after six, really *not* feeling tired . . . My kind Lord Melbourne . . . asked kindly if I was tired; said the Sword he carried was excessively heavy. I said that the Crown hurt me a good deal.' – *Queen Victoria*

The day saloons of Edward VII's royal train (left) *and Victoria's* (right). Below, *the royal family soon after the birth of Princess Beatrice in 1857. From left to right the children are: Alfred; Helen (b. 1846) who married*

The youthful new ruler and her elderly prime minister compared notes after the *longueurs* of the coronation of Victoria, Queen of Great Britain. It had been a long and exciting day, but *not* – as the Queen characteristically emphasized in her journal – really tiring.

Neither did the 19-year-old monarch make any mention in her journal of the historic traditions behind the pomp and splendour. No mention either of the Scottish royal stone of Scone lodged beneath the seat of the coronation chair. Of how the text from the *Book of Kings* – describing King David's annointing by Zadok the Priest and Nathan the Prophet – had been used at every English coronation since that of Edgar the Peaceful in AD 973. Nor of the 'shouts' which were the last echoes of the Anglo-Saxon inauguration of a king by popular acclaim.

As Victoria's long reign progressed, the actual powers of her office – already slight – were to be diminished still further. Yet the Queen herself came to embody the honour and the ancient charisma of monarchy ... modern Europe's oldest institution of government.

When she died in 1901, the American novelist Henry James lamented the passing of 'little mysterious Victoria'. Similarly, to subsequent generations she often appeared a staid and stuffy figure. Yet in reality, Victoria was a passionate and headstrong woman with a powerful zest for life. 'She had a sweet way of laughing at unexpected moments; a silvery, really amused little laugh.' In her youth she waltzed gaily to the music of Johann Strauss; and at the age of 70 – to her delight – she was still able to take to the dance floor.

When she came to the throne at 18, Victoria was indeed a pretty – and determined – young woman. Two years later, when she made use of the residual powers of the Crown to appoint her own Ladies in Waiting, she touched off a famous political crisis known as 'the Bedchamber Question'. The incoming prime minister, Sir Robert Peel, refused

Prince Christian of Schleswig-Holstein; Alice; Arthur; baby Beatrice; Princess Victoria; Louise (b. 1847), who married the Earl of Lorne; Leopold, Duke of Albany (b. 1853); and Edward, Prince of Wales.

to take office while ladies of his political opponents still held any offices in Court. Victoria stubbornly refused to appoint him on these terms, and instead kept her beloved Lord Melbourne in office for two more years.

Later, the Queen was to have disputes with other ministers. Her dislike of Mr Gladstone was particularly notorious, as was her consequent shabby treatment of perhaps the greatest prime minister Britain ever had. However, her conflict with Lord Palmerstone in the 1840s had much more serious political consequences. Palmerstone was foreign secretary in 1848, during Europe's 'Year of Revolutions'. He infuriated the Queen by sympathizing with Europe's revolutionaries against her numerous royal relations.

A hundred years ago, a network of family relationships linked many of Europe's Heads of State in personal loyalty and esteem. By the 1890s, Queen Victoria was at the centre of this network. Alexandrina Victoria had been born on 24 May 1819; the daughter of Edward, Duke of Kent, the fourth son of George III, King of Great Britain and Elector of the German state of Hanover. Her mother, Mary Louise Victoria, was a princess of the House of Saxe-Coburg – one of the branches of the Wettin family. The failure of King George's sons to father any legitimate male heirs put Victoria in the line of succession, and her mother trained her for the monarchy from childhood. Victoria's high morals and sense of duty came partly from this training and partly from her beloved uncle Leopold, who became King of the Belgians in 1831. Her frequent shrewdness, straightforward honesty and occasional moodiness were, however, her own. Leopold and her first prime minister, Lord Melbourne, both became father-figures to Victoria, whose own father had died when she was eight months old. Later, of course, her husband displaced them.

In fact Victoria's marriage in 1840 was planned almost clinically by herself and King Leopold. At one time she had

11

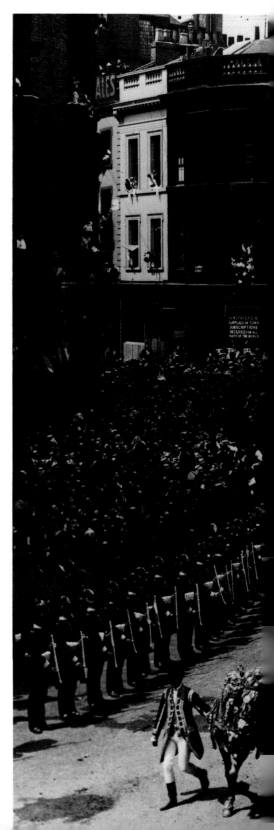

Edward, Prince of Wales, riding beside his mother during the celebrations of her Diamond Jubilee of 1897. Below, the procession passing down King William Street. The celebrations of 1887 had been attended by the crowned heads of Europe; the Diamond Jubilee was a celebration of empire with colonial prime ministers and representatives as the guests of honour. Before setting out from Buckingham Palace, the Queen pressed a telegraph button which flashed a message from her to every part of the empire.

declared against marriage altogether, but – from being merely a suitable consort – her kind-hearted, gifted and handsome cousin, Albert of Saxe-Coburg-Gotha, quickly became an idolized husband. The marriage of their Queen to a German princeling angered many English people. However, the Prince Consort's great tact and obvious devotion to his adopted country eventually won him a grudging respect from contemporaries ... and the title of 'Albert the Good' from posterity.

The royal pair had strong views on the sanctity of marriage and sober habits – perhaps no bad thing consider-ing the disrepute the monarchy had fallen into under the scandalously de-bauched George IV. But we must not forget the Queen's ancestry. Her fore-bearers had had strong sexual appe-tites, and if she confined hers to the marriage bed it was no less powerful. Comments in her diaries, allusive but unmistakable in their meaning, make it apparent that her devotion to Albert was as much for the sexual gratification he brought her as for his more public virtues. It was not because she doted on children that she had so many. In fact, when her first was on the way she complained at the prospect of having her life style hampered by motherhood.

As to the act of birth itself ... Victoria hated it. When she was an old lady she quizzed her granddaughter, Marie of Romania, on her confinement.

'Did they give you chloroform?' she asked solicitously. Marie blushed to admit that they had. The Queen of Romania, who was better known as the poetess Carmen Sylva, believed: 'To bring a child into the world is a moment of such poetical rapture that nothing must be allowed to alloy the ecstasy of its pain.' Victoria had no time for such romantic notions. She heartily reassured Marie that, '... I was only given chloroform with my ninth and last baby (Princess Beatrice) and I assure you, my child, I deeply deplore the fact that I had to bring eight children into the world without its precious aid.'

Despite nine pregnancies in 17 years though, Victoria kept to a tight work schedule until Albert's tragic death from typhoid in 1861 left her shattered with grief. The Queen was 42, and for the next 15 years she virtually withdrew from public life.

During this period the Queen spent much of her time at Balmoral in Scotland, where her confidant was John Brown, a Highland ghillie who had served Albert. Despite his arrogant rudeness to the royal family, Victoria kept him on. Rumour even hinted that she was his mistress. When she was told about this much later, she smiled enigmatically with the comment: 'I did not know I was so notorious.'

More serious were the voices of Republicanism in the air. For a large proportion of Europe, the 19th century was punctuated by revolutions which were repressed bloodily. During the 1840s, even England – for the moment – seemed to be teetering on the brink of upheaval. On one occasion, when Chartists marched through the streets of London to present a petition with more than 1,000,000 signatures demanding constitutional reforms, the troops were held in readiness. But the moment passed, and the fashionable world of privilege giggled somewhat hysterically when it was learned that a subversive wag had added the Queen's name to the Great Charter. Nevertheless, one ineffectual attempt was later made to assassinate the Queen; there were republican demonstrations in Hyde Park; and the humorous papers regularly lampooned the Queen and her Court in cartoons. As the 'Widow of Windsor' continued to draw her parliamentary Civil List of £385,000 and – year after year – live as a recluse, articles appeared demanding: 'What does she do with it all?'

It was ironical that Victoria's return to public favour was, indirectly, due to her heir – Edward, Prince of Wales. The Prince had had his first love affair at the age of 21, and thereafter seemed perpetually under the cloud of his mother's displeasure. Then, in 1878, he nearly died of typhoid and his mother became reconciled to him. The public rejoicings at Edward's recovery afterwards carried the Queen forward on a new wave of public enthusiasm.

From then on, Victoria's popularity never again faltered. She became a symbol of national power and the pride of Empire. In 1887, the Jubilee celebrations for the 50th year of her reign were attended by crowned heads from all over Europe. Among them was the German Kaiser – her son in law; and the German Empress – her daughter Victoria. By this time, and to her considerable delight, the Queen herself was an Empress – of India. The title had been granted to her by parliament at the urging of Benjamin Disraeli, her favourite prime minister. The 60-year Jubilee of 1897 was therefore a great Imperial occasion. Yet the strange little

old lady – who had by then become Europe's matriarch – was still signing government papers to within 10 days of her death four years later. Hers had been the longest reign in English history. When she died she was mourned by the whole Empire, and her passing also marked the passing of an epoch.

The funeral of Queen Victoria of England, Defender of the Faith, Empress of India, ruler of all the British Dominions beyond the seas was indeed a solemn and historic occasion. Yet almost all the host of royals who crowded to be there had some touching or quaint personal memory of the great old lady. For her grand-daughter Marie, it must have been the day when she and her new husband (Ferdinand of Romania) waited in the Queen's room with her . . . to be inspected by her favourite Indian servant, the Munshi. As Marie later recalled:

Left, The Tsar and Tsarina pose with Victoria and Prince Edward during their visit to Balmoral in 1897. The baby is the ten-month-old Grand Duchess Olga. Centre, Victoria with Princess Mary of Teck and one of her grandchildren. Right, Victoria with three future kings: her son, Edward VII; her grandson, George V; and her great grandson, Edward VIII.

'There was a click of a doorhandle and there, on the threshold, stood the Munshi, an Indian idol clothed in gold, with white turban. He remained framed in the doorway . . . simply waiting for those things that were to come to pass. But nothing came to pass. Nando (her husband) had no idea of what was expected of him, and so simply stared at the enigmatic apparition while Grandmama kept hunching her shoulders and smiling as though her smile could make something happen.' Finally Marie broke the spell and shook the Munshi by the hand.

The Munshi – like John Brown before him – occupied the privileged position accorded in medieval times to the Court jester. Brown's license had been his rudeness; with the Munshi it was his

religious practices. In neither case was the Court permitted to inhibit their eccentricities. Even the Queen's royal hosts were required to tolerate these extraordinary royal servants. When Victoria visited the Grand Ducal court of Hesse at Darmstadt, for instance, the Court's major-domo was put to some difficulty to find a 'suitable habitation' for the Indian. The problem was that, wherever he went, the Munshi had the authorization of the Empress 'to slaughter his food within his own

courts'. One cannot help thinking that Victoria must have 'hunched her shoulders' and smiled a good deal to herself as she beheld the turbulence into which she had thrown the otherwise decent, well-ordered Teutonic Court.

The aura of the English Court was felt in many another royal family, through the discrete but often forceful presence of an English governess or nana. Queen Wilhelmina of the Netherlands remembered her governess, Miss Winter, as a 'bold woman' who often emphasized the virtues of the English nation. Nana Matcham, who presided over the German Imperial nursery, was affectionately remembered in later life by the Kaiser's daughter Princess Viktoria Luise. She apparently marked her English loyalty annually, with a solemn little ceremony on the birthday of Queen Victoria. This consisted of a glass of water placed in front of her wine glass. For the royal toast, Nana Matcham reached across the first glass for her wine, 'to signify her loyalty to the Queen across the water'. A century before, English Jacobites, secretly loyal to the exiled descendants of the last Stuart king, James II, had surreptitiously symbolized their allegiance to the 'king across the water' in exactly the same way when called upon to toast Victoria's Hanoverian ancestors.

Given her own German descent, it is not surprising that Victoria was especially close to the German royals. She often addressed William II – who was at her death-bed – as 'my dear boy'. His mother, Princess Victoria, was the Queen's oldest child, and the two were bound by close ties of affection. The fact that this beloved daughter would in due course become Empress of Germany had been an important factor in Queen Victoria's delight when the British parliament – urged by Disraeli – awarded her the title of Empress of India.

The House of Hohenzollern – from which the new Emperor of Germany was descended – took its name from the castle of Zollern in the north of the present-day district of Baden-Wurttemberg. The family began its rise to eminence humbly enough when the great 12th century Holy Roman Emperor, Frederick I, Barbarossa, appointed Conrad of Hohenzollern burgrave of the city of Nuremberg. Early in the 15th century the family were made hereditary Electors (the highest title in the Holy Roman Empire) of the northern province of Brandenburg.

Some 50 years later, Elector Albert Achilles passed a new law of inheritance which was designed to be the cornerstone of the family's future greatness. Traditionally, a German prince's domain was divided between all his surviving sons. Albert Achilles' law, however, ordained that his lands – and those of his descendants – should pass undivided to the eldest son. Conquests and acquisitions of each generation could then accumulate. They included Prussia, once occupied by a Slavic people and outside the frontiers of the Holy Roman Empire. In 1701, Elector Frederick took the title of King *in* Prussia. Twelve years later, at the Peace of Utrecht, Europe's international community acknowledged the upstart royal as King *of* Prussia, and recognized all Hohenzollern lands to be part of this new kingdom.

Meanwhile, the traditional pattern of German inheritance shaped the history of the House of Wettin. Its medieval founders had been powerful men, but by the early 19th century successive divisions of the family's lands had left it with just the small kingdom of Saxony, and a cluster of duchies in Thuringia whose capitals were at Altenburg, Coburg, Gotha, Meiningen and Weimar. Although these areas were nominally sovereign until the German revolutions of 1918, from 1871 they – like many lesser German principalities – were in effect merely semi-autonomous provinces of the Hohenzollern German Empire. However, since these German princes were sovereign, even if only in name, they and their sons made acceptable candidates for the many new European thrones which were created during the 19th century.

The collapse of the power of the Turkish empire in the Balkans produced a situation reminiscent of the position in the Third World following the decline of the European imperial powers since 1945. Then – as now – new nations came into being . . . each needing a new constitution and Head of State. Today, new nations generally choose to be republics, whereas in the 19th century monarchy was still the conventional form of government.

As a result, the first king of liberated Greece was Otto – a prince of the Bavarian royal house; Romania took as a prince, and later king, Ferdinand of Hohenzollern-Sigmaringen – a small princely house distantly related to the German imperial family; and Bulgaria offered a crown to Ferdinand – the son of Duke Augustus of Saxe-Coburg-Gotha. In Ferdinand's case his grandfather had married into the immensely wealthy Hungarian family of Kohary . . . which enabled him to finance his sudden and unforeseen elevation to the monarchial 'club' of Europe.

Nonetheless, several less wealthy branches of the same family also achieved royal status. Leopold of Saxe-Coburg, for example, founded the Belgian royal line; one of his nephews acquired by marriage the title of King Consort of Portugal; while another – Albert of Saxe-Coburg-Gotha – of course became Prince Consort of Great Britain. His wife and cousin, Queen Victoria, also happened to be descended from the Wettins through her mother (Princess Mary Louise Victoria of Saxe-Coburg), and so, in turn, were their children.

Edwardian Era

Previous pages, *Edward VIII in his coronation robes, and the three-feather emblem of the princes of Wales. Below, a house party at Mar Lodge, Abergeldie – the Prince with Lady Arthur Paget and others. Edward was an enthusiastic sportsman. Commodore of the Royal Yacht Squadron, he also won many races on his racing yacht* Britannia *(far right). His love of horse-racing made him still more popular. He won the Derby three times with* Persimmon *(1896; shown right),* Diamond Jubilee *(1900) and* Minoru *(1909). Between 1886 and 1910 his horses won £146,345, and he held an annual Jockey Club dinner at Buckingham Palace.*

Don Carlos, whose opinion of Edward is quoted on the previous page, was not entirely alone in his view of things. The day after the Queen's death, a handbill – headed 'THE ASSERTION' – was fixed to the gates of St James's Palace affirming the rights of 'Mary IV'. This lady was a Bavarian princess who could trace her descent from Charles I. Somewhat to her embarrassment a bunch of ardent eccentrics long maintained her cause in the lesser drawing-rooms of European society.

In January 1901, however, the handbill was removed, and Edward VII – King of Great Britain and Ireland, and of the Dominions across the Sea, Emperor of India – was duly proclaimed to the general satisfaction of his loyal subjects. The queen-matriarch of Europe was dead; she was succeeded by the 'uncle of Europe'.

After 60 years as a prince, the tall and portly Edward – with his grizzled beard and twinkling blue eyes – made a truly avuncular monarch. He was, in fact, an uncle of the German Kaiser (William II);

of the Empress of Russia; of the Queen of Spain; and of the Crown Princess of Romania. Another niece was later to become the Queen of Sweden, and his daughter was to be the Queen of Norway. The Kings of Denmark and Norway and Greece were both his brothers-in-law, and the Kings of Bulgaria and Portugal were his cousins. Further down the royal league, he was also an uncle of the sovereign Grand Duke of Hesse. At his death, in short, Edward VII was the grey-haired and venerable doyen of European monarchy. And yet Don Carlos, if we forget his 'legitimist' fantasies, had had a point. The Prince had undoubtedly had his 'wild ways', and many of his more sober subjects certainly harboured serious doubts as to his suitability to succeed the old queen.

At his christening in 1841, the initials for his two names – Albert Edward – were displayed all over festive London. This cheerful lacework of A.E. monograms prompted one wit, mindful of the habits of previous Princes of Wales, to comment: 'No doubt he will one day be

equally familiar with the other three vowels, I.O.U.' And he was. Affable and easy-going by nature, Edward was forced to spend his boyhood and youth in a rigid and demanding curriculum of study. His serious-minded father, Albert, tried hard to mould his son into the ideal of a modern constitutional monarch. But 'Bertie', despite his earnest efforts, was not meant for desk-work or study.

At the age of 20, when he was sent to the Army camp at Curragh in Northern Ireland for an introduction to the life of an army officer, Bertie had his first love affair. Their son's apparent wayward-ness soon made his parents despair of his suitability for the Crown. Then, news of another escapade took Albert to see his son at Cambridge. The weather was cold and wet and the Prince Consort took a chill. He never properly recovered from this and died shortly afterwards of typhoid. From that moment, Victoria was convinced that the trip – and worry over their feckless son – had killed her beloved husband. As for Bertie, his father's

death was a tragic end to an unhappy childhood. Moreover, his mother's antipathy continued for years, and he was later to confess, 'my mother hated me'.

The Queen was shocked by Bertie's addiction to horse racing, gambling and the delights of fashionable society. Even before he was 30, Bertie was – to his mother's profoundest disgust – cited as just one of the correspondents in a well-publicized divorce case. But then, by a strange quirk of fate, he became the means of reconciling his mother to an increasingly restive public that was irritated by her long, reclusive mourning for the Prince Consort.

On 23 November 1871, following a visit to Scarborough, Bertie contracted typhoid . . . the same disease that killed his father. It seems at first that the Queen could not take seriously the idea that her wastrel son was really in danger of dying. Nevertheless, six days later she travelled up to Sandringham, the country house in Norfolk which had been bought for the Prince with money saved from his allowance during his

minority. Bertie passed the crisis in his illness on 16 December, and the following February a service of Thanksgiving for his recovery was held in St Paul's Cathedral. These dramatic – and public – events inspired a massive resurgence of popular enthusiasm for the monarchy, and from then on Victoria's standing with her subjects was never to be in doubt.

To Bertie's bitter frustration though, his mother never permitted him access to the processes of government despite the family reconciliation. It is perhaps surprising that the serious-minded Mr Gladstone, Victoria's great prime minister, took up his cause. At one point he suggested that the Prince should be made Viceroy in Ireland. But this idea, and many lesser proposals for giving Bertie's considerable diplomatic talents some scope, was curtly dismissed by the Queen. She could only look forward with mournful anticipation to the day when her son would be King . . . and meanwhile refused to inflict him on the country any earlier than was necessary.

Yet the Prince and his beautiful wife Alexandra did discharge one function of monarchy that the Queen would not – and could not. For, whatever other qualities it may have possessed, the old lady's Court was undoubtedly dull. Although the Queen keenly exercised – often to her ministers' irritation – the residual rights of the monarchy to advise, to be consulted and to warn, her role as the leader of the courtly world of the aristocracy went largely by default. It was filled with charm and stylishness by the Wales's. Victoria was even jealous of their popularity, and grouchily dissatisfied with the expansive amiability – and publicity – Edward brought to his part as leader of London's fashionable set. In his 50th year the Prince was called as a witness in the famous Tranby-Croft case, which concerned one of his gaming partners who had been accused of cheating at baccarat. Guest at a constant round of country house parties; friend and lover of a galaxy of beautiful women – of whom the actress Lily Langtry was the most

famous; arbiter of fashion and *bon viveur*, he presided over the 'Edwardian years before his mother's death.

Many of his future subjects, and not only the most puritanical, beheld the activities of 'Edward the Caresser' with profound unease. And yet as a Prince, Edward discharged quite a full programme of more conventional official engagements. A tour of India in 1875, for example, took him across 12,800 km (8,000 miles) of the sub-continent. No doubt the journey was made less arduous by the lavish entertainment of maharajahs, nizams and princes of various ranks, but it was also a necessary royal prelude to his mother's proclamation as Empress of India the following year. As well, Edward cheerfully laid his quota of foundation stones – notably that of Tower Bridge; he was closely involved in the organization of his mother's Jubilee celebrations of 1887 and 1897; and, living up to his name, he presided over a Welsh Eisteddfod and also became the first Chancellor of the University of Wales in 1896.

Before he came to the throne, Edward was even initiated into the full status of a latter-day monarch when an anarchist called Sipido took a pot-shot at him in Brussels, as the Prince left by train for Copenhagen for the Easter of 1900. Edward also knew the Russian capital well, having attended the wedding of his brother (the Duke of Edinburgh) to Grand Duchess Marie in 1874, and the funeral of Tsar Alexander III in 1894. But Edward was an extraordinarily well-travelled prince. Apart from his official and semi-official State Visits, he annually took the 'cure' at German resorts such as Marienbad and Bad Homburg. Wherever he went, his charm and urbanity combined with his exalted social station ensured his popularity with the smart set – the international 'yacht' set as they might be called in the days before jet travel. Among his closest cronies among these royal playboys was Carlos, Crown Prince and later King of Portugal.

Carlos was in fact a distant cousin, descended from the house of Saxe-Coburg through his grandfather Ferdinand, who had married Queen Maria II of the old royal Portuguese family of Braganza. She had been installed as a monarch following an attempt by her uncle, Don Miguel, to usurp the Crown. The supporters of Miguel – who continued as a force in Portuguese politics even after his exile – were excessively right-wing even by the standards of the day, and were opposed to the constitutional liberalization introduced by Maria's father, who was Miguel's elder brother.

Above, *a German cartoon of Edward during the Boer War, captioned: 'Aren't you going to South Africa?' 'No, I must comfort the widows and wives.'* Left, *Queen Alexandra.* Far left, *the Brussels stationmaster overpowers and disarms the 15-year-old would-be anarchist, Sipido, who has fired one bullet from his six-chamber revolver.*

ing with the Fleet in Portuguese waters. In 1902 he again strengthened ties between the old allies with another State Visit, returned by Edward and Alexandra the following year.

However, as a contemporary noted: 'It was unfortunate that, on the very day on which King Edward landed in Lisbon, some cavalry and artillery men to the number of 118 revolted, proclaimed a Republic, and attacked an officer.' Troubles, never very far below the surface of Portuguese politics, were rising ominously. Even Carlos' English connections brought him criticism. People objected that he had accepted the honorary rank of Admiral in the Royal Navy, although he had himself earlier declined an offer of membership of the chivalrous Order of the Garter because of the dispute between the two countries

Left, *Carlos of Portugal; he wrote a distinguished translation of Shakespeare but was less successful as a king.* Below right, *the funeral after his assassination in February 1908.* Centre, *Manoel II of Portugal and his wife.*

Despite the growing liberalist tradition in Portuguese politics however, Carlos – who acceded in 1889 – often acted with confident high-handedness. By 1907, for instance, it was calculated that his personal debt to the national treasury amounted to some £154,000 (more than £2,000,000 in modern values). Critics accused him of extracting these 'loans' by corrupt practices, and even of diverting revenues from state monopolies into the hands of his private creditors. Finally, his prime minister was able to persuade the Portuguese parliament to accept certain royal palaces and the royal yacht *Amelia* as payment of the royal debt ... even though they had all been maintained at public expense for years.

Personally, Carlos was 'a genial, cheery, burly monarch', a considerable

sportsman and – at least according to his admirers – a 'talented artist'. He was as well travelled as his English cousin, and the two had been on the best of terms since Carlos' first visit to England in 1883. Afterwards, he returned on various occasions to stay with his cousin, although on a visit in November 1895 – being by then a reigning monarch – he had been obliged to lunch with Queen Victoria at Buckingham Palace on his way to Sandringham.

These royal contacts were not unimportant, since the two countries were on uneasy terms during the 1880s and 1890s because of rival colonial interests in southern Africa. In fact at Christmas in 1900, Carlos contributed significantly to a bettering of Anglo-Portuguese relations with a cordial reception he held for British naval officers who were serv-

in Africa. But critics also complained, more seriously, that the King of their Catholic country had been infected by the beliefs of the Freemasons as a result of his London contacts. This was not, in fact, improbable as King Edward was certainly a patron of the movement and was inaugurated as Grand Master of the English Freemasons in 1874.

As a conciliatory gesture to his in-creasingly restless people, King Carlos declared an amnesty for political prisoners on 1 January 1901. Three weeks later he was again in London, this time for the funeral of Queen Victoria. There he took part in a significant little gesture of monarchic liberation with the Kaiser and the King of the Belgians. They all stood puffing at their cigars like naughty schoolboys 'by a fireplace in a corridor in Windsor Castle where smoking had always been strictly forbidden'.

Then Carlos was abruptly brought back to reality by news from home, and he had to hurry back to Portugal on 24 January. A bill for the repeal of the sentence of exile on the descendants of Dom Miguel had been defeated by only four votes. It heralded further disturbances. Carlos proved unable to understand or come to terms with the discontent in the country. His cosmopolitan lifestyle and immediate ancestry encouraged a European rather than a Portuguese view of affairs. As we have seen, through his German grandfather Carlos was part of a wide family of north European royals. His mother, the Italian princess, Maria Pia, further widened his outlook, and in 1886 he had married Marie Amelie, daughter of Philippe, Duc d'Orleans.

To their royal relations the Portuguese King and Queen appeared a cultured and affable couple. Carlos, a competent painter and an informed student of oceanography, was also a noted patron of science. The Queen had symbolized her identification with liberal causes by her patronage of a society for the emancipation of women. She had also taken the practical step of enrolling herself as a student of medicine at Lisbon University . . . and insisting on sitting the exams and being passed. It was of course only a symbolic achievement, but it was a powerful symbol for Portuguese women.

Although Carlos and Marie Amelie ranked as impressive sophisticates among European royals, at home they appeared as idle and corrupt parasites. The King's shady financial dealings had brought matters to a head, and a forthcoming parliamentary debate threatened to expose him still further. To avoid this humiliation he suspended the constitution in May 1907, and appointed João Franco as virtual dictator. But by then Carlos was unable to stem the tide of revolt, and in the following February he and his 21-year-old heir – Louis, Duke of Braganza – were assassinated in the streets of Lisbon in a hail of revolver and carbine bullets.

The King's younger son and successor, Dom Manuel, outlasted his father on the throne by less than three years. In October 1910, the murder of a prominent republican precipitated the revolution that had been so long in preparation. Soldiers, civilians and municipal guards joined forces to attack loyal garrisons and the royal palace, while the guns of a warship in the Tagus added to the revolutionary cannonade. Three days of almost constant street-fighting were enough to drive out the timorous young monarch. He eventually reached London *via* Gibraltar, to be greeted by his grandfather, the Duc d'Orleans. Old King Edward, who had been much disturbed by the news of King Carlos' death, was spared the sight of the total collapse of monarchy in Portugal. He had died in the May of that year.

At the start of his short reign in 1901, however, Edward had marked his accession to full royal power with almost childish *pique*. Within weeks of his mother's funeral he began moving through the palaces and ordering the removal of pictures and treasured objects which had been in their places for decades. In particular he cleared the room in which the Prince Consort had died 40 years previously. This had been kept like a mausoleum, unused – indeed untouched – with all his furniture and personal effects as he had left them. To do this was no doubt healthy and understandable, but to sell Osborne House on the Isle of Wight – which his parents had made into a homely retreat for their young family – seemed simply to be taking callous revenge on his own unhappy childhood. Nonetheless, on 16 March 1901, he bade farewell to his eldest son George, Duke of York, and his wife, Princess 'May' of Teck, as they set off on a tour of Australia, New Zealand, the southern African Cape Colony and Canada. For Edward, who had a deep affection for his son and heir, it was a bitter leave-taking. But preparations for his own coronation were soon absorbing his attention.

It was to be a magnificent affair, and the questions of protocol and ceremonial it posed were the sort to fascinate Edward. Like other modern constitutional monarchs with little real power, he was a stickler for formality. At times, one feels, he had a point. A member of the Royal Victorian Order and, on another occasion, a Knight of the Garter had both to be informed by the King of the correct way to wear their decorations. Since these are the two most prestigious honours in the gift of the British Crown, it seems the recipients sometimes took their distinctions a little casually. However, perhaps the royal martinet was going too far when he dispatched an equerry to the orchestra pit in the interval of a performance at Covent Garden Opera House, to reprimand a musician who was wearing a black tie instead of a white one.

Edward's coronation preparations had, however, to be dramatically abandoned with only days to go when the King fell severely ill with an inflammation of the intestine. Dismayed, the nation waited hourly for news of his death. When he made an astonishingly fast recovery, Edward refused to postpone the ceremony to allow the impressive list of dignitaries on the original guest list to attend. Instead, he went to his coronation on 9 August 1901, with few of Europe's royals in attendance . . . but to the heart-felt rejoicings of his own people.

The King did not stop his travels after coming to the throne, but they then took on a new significance. In April 1903, he made the first visit by an English monarch to Italy, being received by Victor Emmanuel; but his

The French newspaper Petit Journal *was fascinated with Edward VII. Top, scene in a London street, recorded by its artist during Edward's illness in 1901. Above,* Edward's departure from Cherbourg after his 1903 French tour. *Right,* at the French grand military review, Vincennes, May 1903. *Far right,* during his visit to Berlin with officers of the 1st Prussian Dragoon Guards wearing regiment uniform.

audience with Pope Leo XIII startled public opinion much more. The King was soon to earn the title of 'Edward the Peacemakers' from admirers, and the bridge-building exercise at the Vatican was entirely in character. Equally dramatic, and of greater significance, was his reception in France.

Anglo-French relations had traditionally been antagonistic since the Middle Ages, but they were particularly hostile in 1900 because of colonial rivalries in Africa. The French press bloomed with vicious cartoons against England and against Edward himself. So, naturally, genial Edward's first major exercise as King was to try and improve matters. Initially, his State Visit of 1903 met with cold indifference from the crowds along the Champs Élysées. But King Edward had his own style of diplomacy. Visiting the Theatre Français that evening, this famous friend of actresses gallantly paid his respects to the renowned Jeanne Granier. In a voice loud enough to carry through the foyer, he carefully enunciated in his best French: 'Ah, Momeselle, I remember how I applauded you in London where you represented all the grace, all the *esprit* of France.' As he had hoped, the remark was being quoted with approval throughout Paris the following day. He continued this gracious line in flattery during his formal speech at the British embassy, not forgetting to mention '*la gloire*'. The next evening, on his way from the Élysée Palace to the Opera, he found his way blocked by cheering crowds shouting '*Vive Edouard!*' and even '*Vive notre roi!*'. In the words of the Parisian press, the visit which had started so inauspiciously ended with popular demonstrations of 'delirious fervour'.

The following year Edward was with the Kaiser for the regatta at Kiel – one of the high events of the social season. The year before his death he made a State Visit to Berlin, and he was also active in fostering good relations with the Russian Empire. Few doubt the important contribution that Edward made to the improvement of Anglo–French relations, nor his standing in the international community. His contemporaries were somewhat uneasy that his socializing diplomacy was often undertaken without due liaison with the Foreign Office; while foreigners got the impression that his influence in his country's government was far greater than it was. The true position of a British monarch in the first decade of the 20th century was more accurately reflected in the crisis over the power of the House of Lords – a crisis which clouded the last months of Edward's reign.

Asquith's Liberal government, wishing to push through a series of major social reforms and having the necessary majority in the House of Commons, was faced with having its legislation repeatedly blocked by the overwhelmingly right-wing Upper House. The one constitutional way out of the impasse was for the King to create sufficient new peers from among government supporters to effectively abolish the veto enjoyed by the Upper House. Of course this would mean the creation of hundreds of new noblemen, and although Edward had enjoyed dispensing lesser honours to his friends he was appalled at having to dilute the aristocracy of England in this way. Perhaps he even reflected wryly that in 1885 the Portuguese administration had legislated to phase out the parliamentary voting rights of hereditary peers . . . and that 25 years later the monarchy there was on the point of collapse. In the event, death released Edward from the decision. His son George grimly prepared to do his duty, but he too was spared when the Lords – rather than admit hundreds of upstarts – voted away their own powers of ultimate veto.

Spared to the last of any serious involvement in the sordid arena of politics, Edward VII instead went to his tomb a symbol of the flamboyant dignity of one of the great epochs of monarchy. His funeral cortege was followed by the German Kaiser, Crown Prince Francis Ferdinand of the Austro-Hungarian Empire, the Kings of Greece, Spain, Portugal, Denmark, Norway, Belgium and Bulgaria. It was, by any standard, a fitting escort.

Imperial Germany

On 26 July 1914, only days before the outbreak of World War One, Prince Heinrich of Prussia – brother of the German Kaiser – had a conversation with King George V of Great Britain. At one point, the King said: 'We shall try all we can to keep out of this and to remain neutral.' When the Prince's report reached Berlin, the Kaiser – confident that he now had a British pledge of neutrality – portentously announced his belief to Admiral von Tirpitz. The Admiral was not impressed. He, like many members of the German administration, must often have wished that their monarch was subject to the same constitutional restraints as his English cousin. He no doubt saw in the English King's remarks merely an expression of personal hope. He knew that no King of England could speak for his government in such a matter. William II dismissed his doubts, saying: 'I have the word of a King and that is good enough for me.' Confident there would be no war, he went ahead with plans for a cruise.

Two portraits of the Emperor: below, he is in the uniform of the Cuirassiers of the Guard. Right, *the inauguration of the German Empire in the Hall of Mirrors, Versailles, on 18 January 1871. The artist shows Bismarck, 'the Iron Chancellor', looking up at King William I of Prussia while officers of the German army hail him as Emperor of a united Germany.*

The Kaiser was never happier than when living out the part of ruler as though in some medieval pageant. He changed his uniform several times a day through a scale of colours which generally culminated in the full dress uniform of the Cuirassiers of the Guard – a snow-white suit, with huge gauntlet gloves, high shining boots and an eagle-crowned helmet. This costume, fitting perhaps for some hero of legend, suited less well the head of a government as the German Kaiser certainly was. The appointment of the Chancellor, Germany's chief minister of state, was in his hands; and the commanders-in-chief of the armed forces were also answerable directly to him ... not to the Reichstag ('parliament') or even the Chancellor.

William II, the third and last monarch of a united Germany, was born on 27 January 1859, the eldest son of Prince Frederick William of Prussia and Princess Victoria of England. A new verse was written for the British national anthem to celebrate the great dynastic occasion:

'Hail the Auspicious morn,
To Prussia's throne is born
A Royal heir!
May he defend its laws,
Joined to Old England's cause,
This wins all men's applause!
God Save the Queen!'

Few could have foreseen the bitter end to this happy dream. In 1859, Prussia was merely the most powerful among a patchwork of German states. In the next 20 years Germany reached European great power status, thanks to the ruthless brilliance of Bismarck, the 'Iron Chancellor'. The title 'Kaiser' was adopted in 1871, when King William I celebrated a crushing defeat of France by Prussia and her German allies by having himself crowned Emperor ('Kaiser') of a united Germany ... in the Hall of Mirrors at Versailles.

Young William's mother, a daughter of Queen Victoria, was convinced of the superiority of English institutions and frankly considered Prussia a backward country. Many Prussians in turn regarded her as infecting her husband with unduly liberal views, and Bismarck was among her enemies. Nevertheless, the young Prince was given a middle-class education, contrary to both the proud traditions of the Hohenzollern House and his own growing self-conceit. After high school and university, however, he went into the guards regiment – where he found himself treated with gratifying deference. The haughty elitism of the Prussian noble and officer class suited him far better than the egalitarian ideals of his mother's household.

'My son has no motive save vanity', noted his mother, as a growing antagonism and distrust soured their relationship. It was fostered by Bismarck, who rigorously excluded Prince Frederick from the conduct of state business but saw in the young Prince a disciple to his policy of Prussian expansionism. William was indeed fascinated by the triumphs of his grandfather's reign. The old man died in 1888, followed three months later by William's father, Emperor as Frederick III, struck down by cancer of the throat. For Victoria, the widowed Empress, it was a bitter end to 30 years of preparation for a more liberal regime. Brutally, her son had troops surround the palace to prevent her removing her private and state papers.

William II had extravagant ideas of the divinity of Kingship and the Imperial destiny of Germany. 'God', he once pronounced, 'would not have taken such great pains with our German Fatherland if he had not yet greater things in store for us'. Obviously, William's enemies were later to label him as the chief architect of World War I. However, his simple principle was to maintain the standing of the monarchy at home and of his country abroad. To do this, military might was essential. Consequently, Prussia's army was soon the strongest in Europe, and William determined to make Germany a major naval power. His patronage of this particular armament drive angered the British, but he protested – perhaps truthfully – that he had no warlike intent. His Chancellor, von Bulow, once summed it up in the words: 'We seek to put no one in the shade; merely to give ourselves a place in the sun'.

Germany wanted a colonial empire, a powerful navy and an influence in Europe to match its growing economic might. Any one of these was itself a feasible objective. However, pursued together in the unsubtle and provocative style of William and his ministers, these policies inevitably forced Germany's powerful opponents together. By 1914 Germany was Europe's most powerful country – both restless and ambitious. It was the world's misfortune that during this period it was also ruled by a restless and ambitious dilettante.

Flattering courtiers had as their motto: 'The Emperor must have sunlight only.' A biographer meanwhile observed: 'As soon as he showed himself to the public he put on the mask of Emperor. When he put it aside there remained a man of fine talents but of moderate education and weak character, vain and wilful through excess of self-consciousness, who liked to surround himself with subservient people

who suffered his not always tactful jokes with becoming respect.' And 'suffer' was the *mot juste*. When the Bulgarian princes, Boris and Kyril, returned from the German military manoeuvres of 1912, they were duly impressed by the army but 'bruised all over from the digs and buffets, jovially conferred on them by the Kaiser, according to his deplorable habit.' The 32-year-old Winston Churchill, who was also a guest at those manoeuvres, had a different comment to make: 'The Kaiser spoke to me with his usual ease . . . with the majesty that no one can deny him.'

Undoubtedly William played the part of Emperor well when he wished to, and he had a remarkable facility of speech – whether in public or private. Too often his fluency led him to commit himself and his ministers to ill-considered policies conceived in the enthusiasm of the moment. At the start of the reign Bismarck had aimed to restrain the Kaiser's influence on policy. A clash was inevitable, and it came when the idealistic young Emperor declared a sweeping series of social measures without first consulting the Chancellor. Bismarck, relying on a cabinet order of 1850, forbade ministers to report to the monarch except in his presence. Furious, William called for the old man's resignation – and got it. There could hardly be a more dramatic instance of the constitutional differences between Britain and Germany. The dowager Empress meanwhile watched with sour satisfaction as her wayward son humiliated her ancient enemy.

Announcing the departure of Bismarck in 1890, the Emperor told the nation that the 'ship of state' would remain on the same course . . . but under a different steersman. Europe's statesman watched apprehensively as the ship steamed on under its talented but unpredictable young captain. The posture was proud, but many recognized beneath it an insecure personality which they attributed to sensitivity about a deformed arm which had embarrassed William from youth.

Yet when he put off the 'mask of Emperor' William could be a considerate host and amiable father. For instance, when the Court at Potsdam was preparing for a visit from Archduke Francis Ferdinand of Austria, an embarrassing point of protocol arose. As the Archduke's marriage was a love match with a lady of low social rank, propriety would be offended if husband and wife were seated together at a conventional long banqueting table. On the other hand, if they were placed according to rank they would be embarrassingly separated by scores of guests. It was the Kaiser who solved the conundrum by suggesting that the dinner be served on small separate tables.

Dinner at home could be still more informal. In her memoires, his only daughter – Princess Viktoria-Luise – recalls relaxed picnics on the country estate at Wilhelmshohe. The family would gather round a wood fire; the children watching potatoes roasting in the ashes while mama cooked omelettes and papa mixed the salad. It was clearly

Wilhelm II seen with Crown Princess of Greece, Empress Frederick, Princess Royal of Saxe-Meiningen and Princess Frederick Charles of Hesse.

a happy childhood – a kaleidoscope of fairyland ceremonies and happy summers spent walking along the Holstein coast, 'through woods and lakes, the villagers coming out of their thatched cottages to greet their Empress.'

In fact the villagers themselves were, more probably, cheering their former Princess. The Kaiserin had been born into the ducal house of Schleswig-Holstein, which was formerly a province of Denmark. When Bismarck was manoeuvring to annex the territory in the 1860s, her father had dared aspire to the dukedom. It was hoped that by the marriage of his daughter to Prince William in 1881, Prussia could placate opposition elements in Schleswig-Holstein. Nor was this the only part of the new, greater Germany where anti-Prussian sentiments could be found.

King George V of Hanover had also dared to oppose the Bismarckian state and, as a result, had lost his realm. Later, the question of the Hanoverian succession caused problems in the Kaiser's family when Viktoria-Luise became engaged to Ernst August, heir to the dukedom of Brunswick and son of the Hanoverian claimant. He refused to relinquish this misty honour, although it was clear to everyone that the once independent kingdom (of Hanover) had become a permanent part of the Prussian state. In contrast, Brunswick itself was one of several semi-independent duchies of the German Empire, and to solve the problem the bridegroom's ageing father finally agreed to renounce his title in favour of his son. The young

31

Above, *on military manoeuvres, the Kaiser and a general enjoy a joke with Count Fürstenberg of Austria; a British observer, Lord Lonsdale, walks towards them from the left.* Left, *with Admirals Tirpitz and Holtzendorff on the imperial yacht,* Hohenzollern. *King George V of Britain and the Kaiser,* right, *at the wedding of Princess Viktoria Luise of Prussia, the two monarchs wearing uniforms of regiments in the other's army;* above right, *riding to take the salute during a military parade at Potsdam, May 1913.*

Duke then entered the Prussian army and so, necessarily, took an oath of allegiance to the Kaiser. The actual cause of the trouble, the claim to Hanover, was discretely not mentioned. Nevertheless, there was much umbrage taken and comment made in 'old Hanoverian circles' that a scion of the ancient house of Guelph of Hanover should swear allegiance to the Hohenzollern King of Prussia.

But Prussian self-respect was also involved in this difficult marriage. According to the British Royal Marriage Act of 1772, no member of the House of Guelph could marry without permission of the head of the family – and that was still the King of England. Viktoria-Luise, ignorant of all this, was apprehensive when informed that she would have to be married 'the English way'. Her proud father, however, had no intention of humiliating himself by asking permission from Buckingham Palace. Instead, he formally notified George V of the marriage. Far from taking offence, the King of England – along with the Emperor of Austria, the Tsar, King Ludwig III of Bavaria, Prince Max of Baden, the Grand Duke of Mecklenburg-Schwerin and others – stood as a godfather to the couple's first child, born in 1913.

This glittering list of sponsors was indeed a pretty emblem of royal reconciliation ... just a year before the Armageddon which was to shatter royal (and not-so-royal) Europe. However, despite this fleeting cordiality, war had been in the European air for some time. In 1908, William had been seriously at odds with Austria, Russia and England. Then, taking advantage of upheavals in Turkey, Austria had annexed the Turkish Balkan province of Bosnia. The Kaiser was angered that Russia supported a Serbian protest against Austria; he was furious that Austria had acted without consulting him, and accused that country of duplicity.

In the same year, when King Edward VII of Great Britain was visiting Freidrichshof, William told a British adviser 'most abruptly' that Germany would not consider negotiations over general arms limitations. Shortly after he gave an interview to the *Daily Telegraph*

which contrived to affront both German and English public opinion, while aiming at precisely the opposite result. He had said that while he, personally, was a friend of England, German public opinion was hostile. In October he had to make a statement to the *Reichstag* that in future he would undertake no such political step of importance without first consulting the Chancellor. He was bitter about this as he claimed that the Chancellor had, in fact, vetted and approved the article himself.

However, William II had the weak person's habit of always blaming others. He did sometimes show more political acumen than his ministers, but he was generally too indecisive to carry his point against them. His uncle, Edward VII, who died in 1910, had writ-

ten: 'My nephew will release the forces of war not as a result of his own initiative, but out of weakness.' True to form, as he signed the orders for mobilization on 1 August 1914, William commented: 'Gentlemen, you will live to rue the day that you made me do this.'

Until the last moment, William seems genuinely to have been convinced that war could be averted. For years he had supposed he could build a world role for Germany based on his own acumen and his royal friendships – notably with 'Nicky', Tsar Nicholas of Russia. Then, in July 1914, Franz Ferdinand – whose wife William had treated so tactfully at his banquet all those years before – was assassinated by Serbian nationalists in Sarajevo. The Kaiser firmly believed, even then, that the commonality of

monarchical sentiments would deter Nicky from coming forward to defend the murderers of a Prince. He utterly misunderstood the strength of pro-Slav feeling in Russia, and failed to grasp that the decision did not, in any case, lie with the Tsar. He sent a stream of telegrams to Nicholas urging him to refrain from mobilizing the Russian army ... and meanwhile prepared to enjoy his Baltic cruise.

War came nonetheless. As it progressed, William proved unable to assert his authority either as supreme warlord or as Head of State. Decisions continued to be referred to him as a matter of form, but – by 1916 – the High Command under Hindenburg and Ludendorff had usurped effective political control. By October 1918 it was clear that Germany's magnificent last offensive had exhausted the nation's war effort. The USA's entry into the war in 1917 had made defeat only a matter of time ... and that time had now come. With the Allies demanding the Kaiser's abdication as a precondition of armistice, and revolution beginning to loom in Germany itself, Ludendorff hastily thrust the reins of power back into civilian hands and left office.

Prince Max of Baden was to be appointed Chancellor. However, even at this stage in the world's affairs, the precise protocol of monarchy had still to be observed. Prince Max's father, as Grand Duke of Baden, was the ruler of one of the semi-sovereign states which made up the German Empire. Not even the Kaiser could confirm the appointment of Prince Max to government office without first obtaining the Grand Duke's permission. Both father and son viewed the prospect with apprehension,

and foresaw only disgrace. Max spoke on the telephone to the old man: 'I had to listen to sorrowful words. The Grand Duke hated the thought that a Prince of Baden should be charged with the liquidation of a lost war. He warned me of the awful consequences for me and my House.' But, however reluctantly, he agreed. The Prince was appointed Chancellor, and duly signed the note to the Allies requesting an armistice. However, he protested to the military authorities that his position as heir to the throne of Baden made it intolerable for him to append his signature to the Deed of Armistice itself.

Thereafter events moved rapidly, bringing in their train awful consequences for the House of Baden. With chaos at home and a frightening desertion rate from the armies in the field, Prince Max felt compelled to accept the Allies' terms. At midday on 9 November he announced that William would abdicate both as Emperor and as King of Prussia, and that the Crown Prince would renounce the succession and a regency council would be formed. But the time had passed for such traditional remedies, as that same afternoon the Berlin crowds were cheering for the Republic.

The Kaiser himself was far away on the Western Front, and events in the capital posed him a dilemma. He could gamble on the loyalty of the troops at hand and try for a counter-coup, or – in the romantic traditions of the ancient German kingship he had so long claimed for his own – he could choose a hero's death at the head of his army in a last, hopeless battle. In fact he stole quietly across the Dutch frontier on 10 November. In so doing he struck a fatal blow to the monarchist cause throughout the German lands. Deserted by their royal leader, the minor princes had no choice but to capitulate and abdicate before the incoming, angry tide of revolution.

In some places the revolutionaries had anticipated events. Early in November 1918, Princess Viktoria-Luise was ill with flu in a room at the castle of Brunswick. On the evening of the 7th, a mob of escaped prisoners broke into the gatehouse; the guards fled and her husband had to slam and bolt the doors to keep the rioters out. The next morning they were back, headed by mutinying soldiers who burst in and demanded to see the Duke. He somehow managed to pacify them. Then, as they left the room, one of them was about to pocket a silver cigarette box. He was stopped by another, presumably senior member of the delegation, who slapped his wrist and said, 'one does not do that sort of thing'.

Above, *this war-time propaganda picture of William II with Field Marshal Hindenburg is captioned 'Deutschlands Stolz', 'the pride of Germany'. After the war and the humiliation of both army and empire, William pestered Hindenburg until the latter finally accepted responsibility for*

The Brunswick revolution was headed by the Spartacist, Auguste Merges, who formed the Brunswick Red Guards. On the afternoon of the 8th, Merges himself led a deputation to the Castle with the news that the Duke had been deposed and government was now in the hands of a 'Workers' and Soldiers' Council'. 'Believe me', responded the Duke, 'it's a great relief to be free of the responsibility.' He and his family were ordered out of the country. A few days later, the Duke and Duchess, with their little daughter Friederike (later to be Queen of Greece), joined Prince Max himself in a special train laid on for them by the new socialist Chancellor in Berlin.

The same high seas that swept away the little throne of Brunswick had begun to run barely a week before at the naval base of Wilhelmshaven, in Kiel. On 30 October the Fleet was seething with rumours that the High Command planned a final, suicidal battle with the Royal Navy. The sailors mutinied, and an attempt to suppress the revolt failed. The following day a Workers' and Soldiers' Council was set up. Its demands hardly amounted to revolution, but they unleashed a massive wave of change nonetheless. The grand Duke of Oldenburg and King Frederick Augustus of Saxony abdicated, and the Grand Duke of Mecklenburg-Schwerin was deposed. These Dukes' titles only dated from the Congress of Vienna in 1815, when the boundaries of Europe had been redrawn after the 15 years of French aggression known to history as the Napoleonic wars. Napoleon, hero of the Republic, had himself crowned 'Emperor' in the presence of the Pope ... and he did not hesitate to make other men 'Kings'. The Congress of Vienna recognized some of these titles, and many of the German princes so honoured came from families which had governed their states as sovereign princes of dukes for generations before Napoleon. Then, in the flood which followed the Great War, they were all swept into oblivion.

In Bavaria, ruled since the Middle Ages by the Wittelsbach family, Maximilian had played a calculating game. Alliance with Napoleon brought him the title of King; defection to the Allies in 1813 made the title secure. His son, Ludwig I, delighted Europe and infuriated Bavarians with his affairs. His most notable was with the Irish adventuress 'Lola Montez', mistress of the elder Alexandre Dumas and also Liszt, the composer. He was deposed in the Revolution of 1848. His grandson, Ludwig II – the extravagant patron of Richard Wagner – moved from eccentricity to near madness in 1886, at which point the Kingdom was placed under the regency of his uncle Luitpold. Uncle retained his influential position even when his younger nephew, Otto, came to the throne in the same year. Otto had been certifiably insane since 1883. He was at last deposed when his cousin, Luitpold's son, was crowned King Ludwig III in November 1913.

Ever since 1871, Bavarian members of the Prussian–German Empire had retained a proud sense of difference and superiority. Then, when Austria–Hungary capitulated to the Allies in the closing months of World War I, Bavarians found their southern frontier suddenly vulnerable to invasion. The peace movement strengthened, and with it Bavarian separatism. The Independent Socialists, traditionally an anti-war party, then became the spearhead of revolution. In the early hours of 8 November, they organized a 'Constituent Soldiers' and Workers' and Peasants' Council', and promptly proclaimed the 'Bavarian Democratic and Social Republic'.

Later that day, King Ludwig – whose eldest son, Prince Rupprecht, was meanwhile completing a brilliant wartime career on the north German front – left Munich with his queen and their daughters. They went first to Berchtesgaden, which later became Hitler's mountain retreat. From there, on 13 November, Ludwig formally issued a proclamation releasing his soldiers and officials from their oath of allegiance to the Bavarian royal house. However, this bucolic old gentleman – for whom the revolution had come as a complete surprise – never did formally announce his abdication.

having advised the Emperor to go into exile. Germany's defeat ended the pageant of her ruling families. Grand Duke Frederick Francis IV of Mecklenburg-Schwerin (above left), *whose uncle married Queen Wilhelmina of the Netherlands, and the Grand Duke of Baden* (above right).

Not so the Kaiser himself, who had been a refugee in the Dutch castle of Amerongen since 10 November. After a lengthy – but characteristic – period of vacillation, the Emperor eventually signed a formal deed of abdication on 28 November. Two days later, the last German king – William II of Wurttemburg – followed suit and also abdicated. His small kingdom, with its capital at Stuttgart, was the product of wily diplo-macy during the Napoleonic era. It had joined the Empire in 1871, but retained its own post office, telegraphs, railways and idiosyncracies of taxation. On 9 November 1918, William II was toppled from his throne by a socialist revolu-tion. Even though moderate forces soon replaced the socialists, news of the Kaiser's abdication no doubt persuaded William to abandon any hopes he might have had of making a comeback.

For years afterwards, the ex-Kaiser still fretted over the circumstances of his abdication. At the time, General Groener had said: 'He should go to the front . . . to look for death. He should go to some trench that is under the full blast of war. If he were killed it would be the finest death possible.' In contrast, however, William's ignominious shuffle into Holland was a betrayal of the ancient traditions of Germanic king-ship he had so long mimicked. Inevit-ably he blamed it on others, saying: 'My decision to leave was against my inner conviction, and was forced upon me by . . . military and political advisers.

On the other hand, Hindenburg – his most senior adviser – denied the claim, despite continuous and petulant re-quests from William. However, in August 1920 he compromised and issued a statement which read: 'His Majesty never deserted the colours . . . A hero's death at the head of his army was impossible because an armistice had already been signed.' Amazingly, this was still not enough to satisfy the pride of the man he still called his 'Kaiser, king and sovereign'. So, in July 1922, the ageing Hindenburg capitulated, and loyally accepted 'overall respons-ibility for the decision of 9 November 1918'. His reward was a grudging letter of thanks from William, who was ap-parently relieved that 'the motive behind my departure has *finally* been explained'.

By this time – thanks to the gener-osity of the Dutch government – the ex-Kaiser was comfortably installed at Castle Doorn. Early in 1919, a kidnap attempt led by an American colonel failed, and thereafter the Dutch – guarding their right of political asylum – refused all Allied proposals of extradi-tion. Forgotten by Europe, William wrote his memoirs – a work about the House of Hohenzollern – and, no doubt a little mournfully, penned a treatise on *Royalty In Ancient Mesopotamia*.

In his lonely Dutch retreat, the age-ing monach also dreamed of the past . . . and even of the future. His daughter records: 'Events in Germany occupied him incessantly, though not to the ex-tent of actually intervening personally. Such thoughts had been banished from his mind forever.' In fact, this was not quite accurate. For instance, a startling passage in the ex-Emperor's will clearly showed that he was never reconciled to the demise of the House of Hohenzol-lern. 'Should God decree,' it runs, 'that I should be recalled from this world at a time when there is no restoration of the monarchy in Germany and that I should go to my eternal rest while in exile, then I am to be provisionally buried in Doorn.'

These sentiments were shared by many in Germany, who looked back nos-talgically to the monarch. In fact, when the Kaiserin died in April 1921, the three dark green coaches of her funeral train were greeted by silent crowds all along the 600-km (370-mile) route from Holland to Berlin. Moreover, the right-wing Nationalist Party of Alfred von Hugenberg also recruited much monar-chist support in the post-war years. Hugenberg's newspapers and industrial wealth were even influential in helping

Two shots of the fallen William II in exile in Holland. The Dutch government made available to him residences first at Amerongen and then at Castle Doorn. The picture below is one of the rare occasions on which he allowed the camera to see his deformed left arm.

Hitler to power, partly because the Nazi leader, so he supposed, might restore the monarchy. Outside Germany there was also a sort of fascination for the fallen royals. For instance, while Crown Prince William was interned on the Dutch island of Wieringen, his duties included work for the local blacksmith. On one occasion, an American journalist appeared, and breathlessly offered the smith 25 guilders for a horseshoe from the royal anvil.

Predictably, after his return to Germany, the Crown Prince was attracted to Nazi politics – even toying with the notion of himself as President and Hitler as Chancellor. Although his other son, Prince Augustus William, was also a zealous Nazi, the ex-Emperor himself had no time for 'upstart politicians'. On one occasion, a visit from Augustus William to the haughty old exile slid quietly into vaudeville.

'My father,' wrote Augustus William, 'treated me as if I did not exist. Unfor-

tunately, I lifted my arm a little, quite unintentionally, out of habit, and was snapped at terribly.'

During his rapid, opportunist rise to power, Hitler himself was quite willing to recruit monarchist sentiment to his cause. In an attempt to obtain a royal seal of approval, Goering was even sent to Doorn. However, this flamboyant emissary was received with cold hostility, not – so far as one can tell – because of his politics, but because 'the man's crude and outspoken manner clashed brusquely with the more staid customs of the Court'. Nonetheless, early in 1939, the ex-Emperor – who had received greetings from King George VI of England on his 80th birthday in January that year – approached the Nazis with an offer to mediate between Germany and England. He got no answer.

William found many causes for bitterness in his twilight exile. Even his loving and loyal daughter Viktoria Luise cooled a little when her father

remarried – and that below his station – within a year of the Kaiserin's death. The old man also continued to rail against Prince Max of Baden for forcing him, as he saw it, into abdication not only as Kaiser but also as King of Prussia ... something he had never intended. To him, Max was always a Prussian general who had betrayed his class and his King.

In the end though, the army itself delivered William – the failed warlord – a bitter-sweet present. News of the fall of France, and its ratification at a signing in the same railway carriage which had been used for the Armistice ceremony of 1918, brought tears to his eyes ... whether of joy or humiliation is not recorded. Yet as he lay dying on 4 June 1941, he may have recalled with pleasure how the young soldiers of the *Wehrmacht* – tramping through 'neutral' Holland weeks before – had crowded into his room at Doorn to shake their fallen Emperor by the hand.

Habsburg Twilight

In the year 1908, Francis Joseph II celebrated the 60th year of his reign as Emperor of Austria. At a grand reception in the Marie Antoinette Room of Vienna's Schönbrunn Palace, the guests included the Kaiser, Prince Regent Luitpold of Bavaria, King Frederick Augustus of Saxony, King William II of Wurtemberg, the Grand Dukes of Mecklenburg and Oldenburg and many lesser dignitaries, among them the Mayor of the Free Hanseatic Town of Hamburg. These representatives from northern Germany were paying nostalgic respects to the distant days when all the German lands had acknowledged the supremacy of a Habsburg Emperor.

Even at the apogee of its power, Habsburg supremacy had been little more than theoretical, and since 1806 the head of the family had borne no loftier title than 'Emperor of Austria'. Yet in many ways the 78-year-old Francis Joseph represented a dynasty whose influence had decisively shaped the history of the Germans, and even of Europe itself.

The family traced its ancestry back to the 10th century, and assumed its name in the 12th century from the Castle Habsburg, near Aargau in modern Switzerland. Its lands then grew steadily until 1273, when Count Rudolph IV was elected head of the Holy Roman Empire. In his 18-year reign Rudolph was unable to do much for the Empire, but he managed to establish his family in Austria, Carniola and Styria – the heartlands of its wealth and power for the next 600 years. From the coronation of Frederick of Habsburg as Emperor Frederick III in 1452, the family kept its

Francis Joseph, Emperor of Austria (left and previous pages), *came to the throne in 1848. The heir to the great Habsburg tradition, symbolized by the imperial orb of 1612* (previous page), *willingly authorized ruthless reprisals against the revolutionaries of 1848. But the imperial regime was attacked by nationalist politicians throughout the empire.*

grip on the Holy Roman Empire until the demise of that institution in 1806. During that period, the family acquired the Crowns of Bohemia and Hungary; in 1804 Francis II assumed the title 'Emperor of Austria', and two years later he renounced that of Holy Roman Emperor.

In 1814–15, the Congress of Vienna – which settled Europe's boundaries after the Napoleonic wars – confirmed extensions of Habsburg power into Italy. Next, the dynasty competed with Russia for influence in the Balkans as the power of the Ottoman Empire waned. Finally, in 1867, the Habsburg lands were reorganised as the Austro–Hungarian dual monarchy. From then on, Francis Joseph – Emperor of Austria, King of Hungary, and Duke, Count or monarch of a score of other lands besides – was in control of an Empire vast in extent, but dangerously diverse in language, religion, nationality and tradition.

Periodically, the turmoil seething close below the surface of the Empire burst into open rebellion against the 'master races' – the Germans and Magyars – who made up the bulk of the Imperial Civil Service. The cosmopolitan population of Vienna, the Imperial capital, itself reflected the diversity of the Habsburg lands. At the reception in 1908, few of the more observant guests could have supposed that the ageing autocrat and his successors would be able to hold the balance between the national factions for much longer. In

the event, the disaster which finally crumbled the ramshackle Empire also caused the ruin of old-time Europe.

Francis Joseph was 18 when he came to the throne in 1848 – the 'Year of Revolutions'. From the first he was a willing tool of the reactionary factions at Court, and throughout his 69-year reign he held on firmly to this political stance. He presided blithely over the long, starlit twilight of old Vienna. In that doomed, romantic era, 'Society' people danced carefree to the music of the Strauss brothers, flocked in their fashionable attire to the Cafe Sacher, and preened themselves in boxes at the operetta. Meanwhile, a whole new class of merchant nabobs built palaces on the spacious boulevard of the Ringstrasse, where the city walls had formerly stood. Outside this charmed circle, however, clustered the tenements of the restless urban poor, while abroad, the Habsburg's Empire was in stumbling decline.

As the aristocrats waltzed and curt-sied in Vienna, rival nationalisms tore relentlessly at the seams in the patch-work of lands which owed allegiance to the Habsburg family. Finally, in 1866, its influence in German affairs was shattered when Austrian forces were routed at Sadowa by the Prussian army of Bismarck and King William I. None-theless, as the century drew on, the mellow, bearded features of the Em-peror remained for many a comforting symbol of continuity. Whether as the focus of the dazzling etiquette of Court ceremonial, as the reviewer of his troops in resplendent dress uniforms or – like some patriarchal squire – simply pottering about his estates, Francis Joseph embodied the unchanging spirit of European privilege. Like a rosy haze, the Emperor's familiar autocracy rein-forced the nostalgic *gemutlichkeit* with which the middle classes were content to regard the turbulent waters of social and political change.

Ignorant, like his ministers, of how to calm the brewing storm, Francis Joseph laboured at his paperwork and meddled in administrative minutiae with ineffec-tual thoroughness. For example, his admirers fondly recounted how a sol-dier once gained a private audience with the Emperor, hoping for redress of some barrack-room injustice. After a full and sympathetic hearing the All Highest pronounced: 'I really do not see what I can do; surely you know some sergeant with influence.' Clearly, atten-tion to detail is a hallmark of greatness only in those already great.

Above left, William II, *Emperor of Germany, reads the address of eulogy. Celebration souvenirs included a montage of photo-portraits of the Emperor at various ages* (above right). *The dynasty's name castle, Habsburg Aargau, can just be seen at the top right of the picture.* Right, *Francis Joseph in his favourite clothes; hunting jacket and* Lederhosen.

Yet, such pettifogging concern for the unimportant helped distract the Emperor from his incompetence in great affairs . . . and the unhappy scenario of his private life. In 1854, he had married the 17-year-old Elisabeth of Bavaria. She was an intelligent and kind-hearted woman of arresting beauty, but she was also quite incompatible with the passionless, mediocre temperament of her husband. After 1860, oppressed by the stuffy formality of the Court, Elisabeth spent much of her time abroad, chiefly on the island of Corfu. With her customary kindness however, she also recommended a discrete surrogate wife to her husband. As a result, for some 20 years Frau Katherina Schratt, an actress with the Burgtheatre, was – with the approval of the Empress and the connivance of her own husband – the Emperor's homely solace.

Meanwhile, two years before the Empress Elisabeth made her unconventional departure, the dynasty had been blessed by the birth of an heir. No doubt encouraged by his strange home life, the blond, handsome Archduke Rudolf soon grew into a profligate young rake. Marriage to Princess Stephanie of Belgium did little to steady him. Assisted by Loschek his valet and Bratfisch, the cabby he employed when the use of a palace coach would have been indiscrete, he continued his wild career of drinking and womanizing. Tactfully, the file on his escapades at police headquarters did not record that he had contracted gonorrhea; nor the even more important fact that – during the year 1888 – the heir to the throne had also lost his heart to a 17-year-old called Marie Vetsera.

Sometimes the lovers met in Vienna's Grand Hotel, sometimes in Rudolf's apartments in the Hofburg, and sometimes in a quiet spot in the Prater Park. Marie, the daughter of a minor Hungarian aristocrat, passionately returned the Prince's love. In January 1889, the two exchanged love tokens – Rudolf's was an iron ring ominously inscribed 'United in Love until Death'. By this time Marie was pregnant, and on the 27th the Prince had a long interview with his father at which the Cardinal Archbishop of Vienna was also present. The young man was undoubtedly des-

perate, and it has been suggested that he hoped for an annulment of his marriage. However, at a formal reception in honour of the Kaiser's birthday at the German embassy that evening, he seems to have avoided the Vetseras and their daughter. Indeed, he spent the night with Marie Kaspar – another of his mistresses.

About noon the next day – breaking a second appointment to meet with the Archbishop – the distracted Rudolf drove out to Mayerling, a hunting lodge in the Wienerwald about 20 miles from the capital. Bratfisch followed on with Marie Vetsera. The following day, 29 January, Rudolf excused himself from a night on the town with two of his friends. The next morning he surprised his valet at 6.30 by emerging fully dressed from his bedroom, asking not to be disturbed with breakfast for at least another hour. At 8.15, when neither Rudolf nor Marie had answered repeated calls, the servants eventually broke down the door and found the lovers lying on the bed. Marie was virtually naked and had been dead for several hours; Rudolf was dressed as he had been some two hours earlier. Both had been shot through the head.

Nine years later, the Imperial House suffered yet another blow when the Empress, Rudolf's mother, was shot dead in Geneva by an Italian anarchist called Luccheni. Indeed it seemed that the hand of Fate was raised against the family . . . but when it next struck, the whole of Europe tottered.

After the death of Rudolf, Archduke Francis Ferdinand, the Emperor's 26-

year-old nephew, became heir to the Habsburg throne. However, he made a morganatic marriage with a Czech lady called Sophie Chotek (who was created Princess of Hohenberg) and – largely because of the social conventions at Court – withdrew with his wife from the business of government. From the sidelines, though, he viewed with unease the government's high-handed treatment of the powerful national aspirations in the Empire, and favoured reforms which appeared to include a separate Croat kingdom. Predictably, this earned him the enmity of both Pan-Serbian fanatics and conventional Pan-Germanists; while his support for the Christian Socialists' universal suffrage campaign also angered landowning interests, notably in Hungary. Such a man could hardly expect to survive long in the perfidious atmosphere of the multinational, revolution-ripe Habsburg Empire. He was duly assassinated in Sarajevo on 28 June 1914 by 19-year-old Gavrilo Princip, who instantly became a Serbian national hero. The Austro-Hungarian foreign minister immediately made demands on Serbia which amounted to an ultimatum, and Russia mobilized in support of her little slav neighbour. As a result, Germany declared war on Russia and, to protect its rear, on France – which was attacked through Belgium. To defend France and Belgium, Britain then declared war on Germany. So, by the middle of August 1914, the divisions within the Empire of the Habsburgs had opened up a crevasse that engulfed Europe.

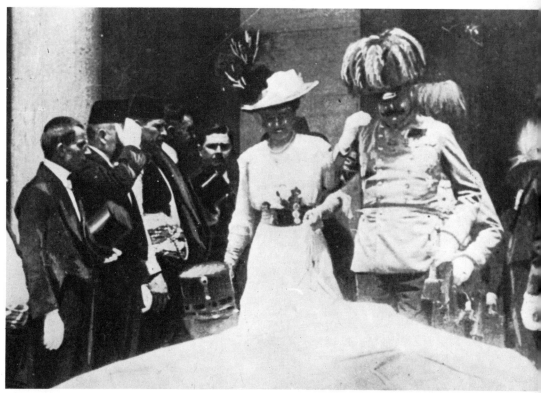

Prince Rudolf (left), *with* (inset) *his mistress, Baroness Marie Vetsera, whose portrait is taken from a locket found on the Prince's body after their deaths. Archduke Francis Ferdinand and his wife are pictured* (right) *minutes before their assassination at Sarajevo on 28 June 1914.*

The same crevasse also swallowed up the Empire without trace. Czech regiments had begun deserting from the Imperial army, early in the war, and as it drew to a close – in October 1918 – Poland, Czechoslovakia and Hungary all declared their independence. Meanwhile, the old Emperor had died in 1916, two years before the ruin was complete. He was succeeded by another grandnephew, the last Habsburg Emperor, Charles I. No ruler could have held on to the inheritance that was his. Although he had shown himself a skilful military commander, and was married to a beautiful and ambitious wife, it seems – insofar as any event in history can be so – that the collapse of his Empire was inevitable.

Charles acceded to the throne on 21 November 1916, and at once decided against an Austrian coronation on the

Above, *Charles, the last Habsburg emperor, and his wife, Zita of Bourbon-Parma. Far right, Charles, crowned king of Hungary. He wears the 11th-century robe and crown of St Stephen. The crown, given by Pope Sylvester II to Stephen I Arpad (d. 1038), saint and king, became the mystic symbol of Christian Hungary's nationhood. After World War II it was smuggled to the USA.*

grounds of expense. However, he eventually was crowned in Budapest with the numinous regalia of St Stephen. The ceremony over, he conformed to ancient tradition by mounting a charger – while still crowned and robed – and ascending to the top of the Royal Hill. There, he levelled his sword symbolically to the four points of the compass . . . rarely can the majestical rituals of monarch have proved so futile.

As he surveyed the situation of the Empire, it was obvious to Charles that peace was imperative. He was horrified by the ignoble brutality of the war, and disgusted by the behaviour of war profiteers – whose money he hoped to confiscate with the cessation of hostilities. He resisted German demands to use Austro-Hungarian ports for the waging of unlimited submarine warfare for as long as he could, and was rewarded with a visit to Vienna by William II in February 1917. However, this did little to stiffen the Emperor's warlike resolution, and in the months that followed he even attempted to negotiate secretly for peace with the Allies. In

this, his go-between was Prince Sixtus of Bourbon Parma, his brother-in-law, and at that time an officer in the Belgian army. Charles recognized that, for France to agree to peace, Germany would have to concede parts of the disputed territories in Alsace and Lorraine. In one characteristically straightforward letter to Prince Sixtus, Charles admitted the justice of some of the French claims in these areas.

When the French government published this letter in April 1918, the Emperor was instantly ostracized by his royal allies. In an attempt to mend bridges, he and Zita made a State Visit to Sofia and Constantinople. They were icily received by King Ferdinand of Bulgaria, although Crown Prince Boris gave them a friendly welcome. In Constantinople, the Sultan's chief minister was prepared to let bygones be bygones. However, a planned visit to Berlin never took place. The Austrian army's defeat by the Italians at Vittorio Veneto instead led to unconditional surrender on 3 November 1918. Eight days later, Charles – who had never taken the oath

to the Austrian constitution – abdicated. Early the next year a hostile regime forced him and his family into exile in Switzerland, where the Villa Prangins – just over the border from Austria – was made available to them.

At 32, Charles faced an uncertain future, but his Empress was determined that they should not forget their past. Zita, the daughter of Duke Robert of Parma, had married Charles in 1911. The following year she gave birth to their heir, and went on to be the mother of a large family. She had great influence over her husband and urged him to regain the throne of Hungary – of which he was the crowned King. 'As long as a drop of Habsburg blood survives, a Habsburg will return – so long as you do not abdicate,' she urged forcefully. However, the Hungarians had set up a republic in the meantime, and between March and October 1919 this was run by communists under Bela Kun. Then a Romanian army overthrew Kun, and when it withdrew a new regime was proclaimed with Admiral Nicholas Horthy as Head of State and Regent.

Late in March 1921, Charles slipped across the border into Austria carrying his passport and disguised as a Portuguese gardner from the Villa Prangins. From there he smuggled himself into Hungary, where he planned to 'take over' the government from the admiral. Armoured in the legitimacy of his cause, and convinced of the loyalty of his people, the would-be King refused supporters' urgings to allow some loyal regiments to march with him. Soon after, his gentlemanly demonstration ended in fiasco when Horthy firmly persuaded him to return whence he had

come. But he refused to abandon hope.

In the light of Charles's actions, the Swiss government began to be uneasy about their guest. They regretted their generosity in providing him a haven, and requested that he and his family leave Swiss soil by January 1922. The Habsburg did indeed comply with this order, but not before Charles had embarked at his wife's urgings on a second mad-cap escapade. On 19 October, piloted by two loyal Hungarian airmen, the royal couple returned to their country aboard an old German Junkers warplane. Their route took them over

Vienna, where the Habsburg eagle emblazoned in tiles on the roof of St Stephen's Cathedral seemed to urge them on to great things. This time, once he had landed on Hungarian soil, Charles agreed to use troops. His forces were easily defeated and so Charles and Zita returned once more to Switzerland before being taken – on a British warship – to Funchal in Madeira. There, on 1 April 1922 – with his wife and family almost reduced to penury – the last of the Habsburg Emperors died of pneumonia.

Charles maintained his rights to the last and his wife upheld them on behalf of her children. Excluded from their homeland by a law of 1919 which banned all Habsburgs who maintained the family claims, they settled at first in Belgium. Between the wars, Otto von Habsburg – who now insists 'I am not a claimant to the Throne' – received two tentative approaches on the possibility of restoration. One came from the Austrian Christian Socialist Party; the other, in 1932, came from Prince Augustus William Hohenzollern. In his capacity as a Nazi Party member Prince Augustus was acting on behalf of Adolf Hitler, making preparatory sketches for the 'Anschluss' of 1938. Both approaches were clearly opportunistic, and both were refused.

However, soon after the outbreak of World War II, Otto made his way via Lisbon to the USA. There he tried, without success, to raise an Austrian legion to fight against Germany. After the war he returned to Europe, married Princess Regina of Saxe Meinigen in 1951, and settled at Pöcking, Bavaria, in 1954. He chose Bavaria for the simple reason that it was 'the most convenient place close to Austria which could be found'. The exiled Habsburg's residence soon became something of a centre of pilgrimage for Austrian monarchists, and was irreverently dubbed 'Pöckingham Palace' by Bavarian wits. Nonetheless, Otto – adopting the style of 'Dr

Habsburg', without even the 'von' – soon renounced his claims. In response, the Austrian legislature finally rescinded the ban on his return to the country in 1966.

Since he became plain Dr Habsburg, Otto has established a large reputation for himself as lecturer and writer on international affairs. As a convinced European he is vice-president of the Pan-European Movement, and sees the supranational character of the old Habsburg Empire as a forerunner of the king of truly international polity which he believes must be formed. He has a cheerful and confident family of five daughters and two sons, but of course there is no heir – no 'Crown Prince'. It seems that the age-old saga of the Habsburgs as a dynasty of rulers is now at an end. As the doctor himself has said: 'Legitimacy is so terribly intangible that it never survives the generation which has seen its end.'

Above left, *the Habsburg eagle on the roof of St Stephen's Cathedral, Vienna;* below left, *the exiled Charles in the old German warplane in which he flew to Hungary in a failed bid to recover his crown.* Above, *Dr. Otto Habsburg, son of the former Emperor, gazing into Austria from Germany at the Steinpass. In the late 1970s he adopted German nationality to fight in the elections for the European Parliament.*

Tsar and Revolution

༺༺༺༺༺༺༺༺༺༺༺༺༺༺༺༺༺༺༺༺༺༺༺༺

Generally speaking it is true to say that nostalgia appeals because it takes us back to a kind of childhood where everything seems clear and beautiful. Those who feel nostalgic for the royalist past are also able to identify themselves with the seemingly heroic, glittering figures of kings and emperors, queens and tsarins, whose privileged positions and assurance of manner apparently put the world at their command. In reality, of course, life was rarely as glittering or assured as the dreamers of romantic royal reveries would like to believe.

༺༺༺༺༺༺༺༺༺༺༺༺༺༺༺༺༺༺༺༺༺༺༺

In the childhood memoirs of Queen Marie of Romania – who was a granddaughter of Queen Victoria – are contained all the ingredients for even the most hard-headed realist to indulge a little in flights of naive royal nostalgia. Marie describes in detail her visits to the Court of Tsar Alexander of Russia. She tells us how the Tsar loved to share the children's games, and would often bounce trampoline-style with them on the safety netting under the masts and rigging set up in the gardens for the young Princes' sea-cadet exercises. Although history regards Alexander as a nervous reactionary, and the fairy-tale Court he presided over was fated to crash in bloody ruin around his son Nicholas 40 years later, the sparkling, joyous atmosphere of her childhood visits was to remain with Queen Marie all her life.

Marie's memoirs further record how the imperial palaces breathed their own 'quite special odour; a mixture of turpentine and Russian leather, of cigarette smoke and scent'. It was a child's paradise, where 'everybody loved you and gave you things to eat, or hung lovely little lockets set with precious stones around your neck.' When you reached your room, it was to find 'there, on the centre of the table, two dishes, one with sweets, the other with biscuits . . . nowhere else in the world were they so good'.

If you went for a walk in the park, 'as you stepped over the terrace down into the gardens' there stood a group of sailors, deputed to be your protectors and companions, 'all smiles with some little surprise for you; a bunch of wild strawberries, a wonderful stick half peeled as though a white ribbon had been wound round it, a little wooden flute, a hoop and what-not else'. And in the surrounding parkland there were lakes and sand pits, a model cottage and model farms with their own live animals, to explore.

Especially for a child, the ceremonies of the Court were a dazzling theatre of colour and make-believe: 'Byzantine in splendour with all the mysterious gorgeousness of the East.' The ladies wore simple white satin tunics and, over them, 'amply cut velvet robes, with trains and wide hanging sleeves . . . heavily embroidered in silver or gold and every colour of the rainbow'. On their heads they wore veiled halo-shaped 'cacoshnics' 'so that every woman appeared to have been crowned'. In those days, 'the processional entry of the Russian Imperial Family into festive hall or saint-haunted church, was a picture once seen never forgotten'.

Yet in reality, all this glory was but the gilded pinnacle of a pyramid founded on privilege and held together by oppression. It was neither comfortable, nor polite, to mention in these gilded halls the Third Section of the Tsar's chancery – more ominously known as the Okhrana. This was the ruler's secret police, only outdone in efficient ruthlessness by its communist successors, the Cheka, OGPU, NKVD and KGB. In view of what has happened since the Revolution of 1917, it may be necessary – but cynical – to conclude that the Russian people are only happy under a tyranny. Ironically, in the years before, 'liberty' had been the watchword for generations of revolutionaries.

The Russian Tsar was a true autocrat. At the close of the 19th century, the effective power he wielded was more absolute than that of many medieval European monarchs. In 'All the Russias', the right to make laws belonged exclusively to the Crown. There was indeed a State Council, but it had only an advisory function. And naturally – as there was no representative legislative assembly – government ministers reported directly to the Tsar . . . but he was in no way bound to take their advice. To maintain the rigid *status quo*, a strong police force was considered essential to the system. The police controlled citizens' rights and liberties, and supervized the internal passport system which effectively controlled all people's movements in Russia. Predictably, the Tsar's government was corrupt from the highest ranks of the administration down to the lowest levels of provincial bureaucracy. Nothing could be achieved without bribes.

Meanwhile, the peasantry was traditionally loyal to the Tsar, whom they referred to as 'little father'. The majority of people believed that it was not the Tsar himself who was responsible

Far left, *Nicholas and Alexandra at the 1913 tercentenary celebrations.* Above, *during a royal progress through the Ukraine.* Centre left, *a ceremonial chair emblazoned with the double-headed eagle.* Left, *detail of Paul I's throne in Pavlovsk Palace.*

for their miseries, but his corrupt agents. They also recognized, in the words of the old proverb: 'Heaven is high and the tsar is a long way off.'

Nonetheless, by the end of the 19th century even the age-old loyalty of the peasantry had begun to falter. At the time, Russia's industrial investment was being financed by the export of grain. But as world grain prices tumbled under the impact of American professionalism in exploiting the prairies, the Tsar's government had to increase exports in order to maintain foreign earnings. As a result, many parts of the country at times suffered under near-famine conditions. In fact, three years before the accession of Nicholas II, a much-travelled English

Member of Parliament wrote: 'In no other country in the world is poverty to so great an extent the characteristic of the people as in Russia.'

The much-vaunted 'Liberation of the Serfs' by Alexander II in 1861–2 had, in fact, barely improved their lot . . . and in some cases actually worsened it. The peasant had indeed been granted the right to purchase land – up to half the area he or she had formally worked as a serf – but the annual redemption payments due to the landlord proved crippling. Moreover, the peasant population was increasing, but the amount made available by the lords for purchase was not. Nor could a peasant leave the land for permanent work in the towns, as the new, powerful village communes were no more eager to lose their labour force than the landlords had been. Finally, while the semi-slave status of the serf had been abolished, he or she remained a second-class citizen before the law. For instance, courts could still sentence a peasant to corporal punishment, but the penalty did not apply to other sections of the population.

Although the peasant 'problem' was a time-bomb ticking away slowly against the foundations of Russia's whole future, more dramatic events were happening on the surface. During the 19th century, Russian society had become much more complex. Increasing contacts with Western liberalism had long been shaping new opinions, and the educated classes were clamouring more and more insistently for a share in government. Even the industrial work force – still a small fraction of the total population – was beginning to have an unexpectedly heavy impact in the cities.

In 1894, at the age of 26, Nicholas II came into this troubled inheritance. He had been brought up in awe and fear of his father, who viewed him with good-natured contempt and had made no attempt to introduce him to the workings of government. In fact Nicholas would, perhaps, have made an adequate junior officer in the Tsarist army. His was a short and unimpressive figure, and he had been advised to appear in public on horseback whenever possible. Nicholas' mind never matured to his responsibilities, and the cataclysmic events that punctuated his reign received little or no mention in his diary. In contrast, the pleasant commonplaces of his domestic life – walking the dog, picking mushrooms, cycling excursions, etc – are all fully recorded.

In the words of one historian: 'Nicholas was a negative character, commonplace in mind, weak of will and

fatalistic of temperament. He was thrust into the blinding light of great events and is saved from complete insignificance only by the macabre pathos of his end.' And yet, according to the same source, 'no Russian emperor was more completely possessed by his prerogative as autocrat'. However, like many weak men, Nicholas was afraid to delegate his duties. He employed no private secretary, himself sealed the envelopes containing official records of his decisions, and rejected all advice that was not accompanied by flattery.

Like all the Romanovs, Nicholas had a winsome charm which he turned on all who came his way – from ministers of state to grooms of the chamber. And yet, as one of them quite simply put it, 'You could not rely on him'. Often, considerate courteousness proved a prelude to disfavour. For instance, a minister who left an audience with approval for a policy might find it countermanded only hours later; another, received with attentive kindness, could be informed next day by Imperial courier – or even by the morning newspaper – that he had been dismissed. Strangely, these frequent deceits were not felt by Nicholas to be betrayals or unfair dealings. From his viewpoint, all the people of Russia were his servants, and should accept his decisions passively. In the words of one official, 'he lacked the capacity for becoming attached to those who surrounded him and parted with them without sorrow'.

In fact, Nicholas believed he had a simple – and divine – mission to pass the Tsar's autocratic power on to his son intact. Just how this was to be achieved in the hurly-burly of day-to-day politics was, however, less clear. The sudden death of his father from kidney disease had left him aghast. 'I am not prepared to be Tsar,' he said. 'I never wanted to be one. I know nothing of the business of ruling. What is going to happen to me – to all of Russia?' Perhaps, predictably, the answer to the new Tsar's question was simply that he was to be dominated by more powerful personalities – his mother, strong-minded ministers, and, later, his wife Alexandra Feodorovna.

The Tsarina was the daughter of Grand Duke Louis IV of Hesse and Princess Alice, a daughter of Queen Victoria. Christened Alix, she had been brought up in Kensington Palace under the supervision of the old Queen. Her personality had thus been shaped by a potent combination of the tastes of aristocratic English Victorian womanhood and the royal pretensions of a petty German Court. Nicholas had married Alix against his parents' will. At the time she was a Protestant, but she later converted to the Orthodox faith and became a passionate devotee. She also took a Russian name.

The mystic panoply with which the Orthodox Church endowed the Imperial autocracy fascinated the highly-strung Empress. Shy, reserved and seemingly arrogant, she was never a popular Tsarina. Nonetheless, she and Nicholas had an idyllic family life of homely simplicity amidst fabulous wealth. They shared it with their adored children – Olga, Tatiana, Maria and Anastasia – then finally the long sought-after son, Alexei. Throughout the mounting crises of the reign, Alexandra bolstered up her husband with her own bounding – if entirely unwarranted – confidence. In 1913, when the tercentenary of the Romanov dynasty was celebrated – in the capital at least – to the cheers of vast crowds, the Empress complacently observed: 'The Tsar's ministers are constantly worrying him with threats of revolution . . . and here we need merely to show ourselves and at once their hearts are ours.' Yet, to those very crowds, she was that German woman'.

The reign of Tsar Nicholas II had begun with a thudding downbeat. In January 1895, he met representatives of the provincial councils which had been established in the 1860s to encourage more autonomous local government – and which had been obstructed ever since by the Ministry of the Interior. Understandably, these people were hop-

Left, *Nicholas aged 22.* Right, *his children, from the top: Olga (born 1895), Tatiana (1897), Marie (1899), Anastasia (1904) and Alexei (1904). Below, Olga, Tatiana and Marie with toys made for them by their father. Nicholas, like his father, also commissioned fabulous Easter gifts for his wife from the court jeweller, Fabergé* (see chapter title-page).

ing for a fresh start, but Nicholas off-handedly swatted their aspirations. 'It is known to me,' he announced, 'that . . . some persons. . . have been carried away by senseless dreams of participation . . . in the affairs of government. Let all know that . . . I shall preserve the principle of autocracy as firmly and as undeviatingly as did my father.' Two days later, during a private discussion, a right-wing, 'establishment' historian was heard to remark: 'The Romanov dynasty will end with Nicholas II. If he has a son, the son will not reign.'

However, as well as prophecies of doom surrounding the new Tsar, there were also bloody omens. One of the first came on 18 May 1896, four days after the majestic coronation, when 500,000 people gathered on the Khodynka Field (now Moscow's airport) for the customary distribution of royal *largesse*. Because of incompetent crown control, a stampede broke out in which more than 120 people were killed. That evening, Nicholas – who was 'slightly unwilling' – followed his ministers' advice and attended a ball at the French embassy with his new wife. The Tsar's apparent indifference to the fate of his subjects was, of course, a propaganda gift to his enemies.

In the foreign affairs field, the Tsar had inherited a secret treaty with France. So, in the summer of 1896, he made a State Visit to Paris. *En route,* the Romanovs stopped off at Balmoral, where a two-week holiday with Queen Victoria and her family was the occasion of many happy snapshots.

Back at home, though, clouds were gathering. The turn of the century in Russia witnessed an epidemic of student strikes which welded the rapidly growing Socialist Revolutionary Party into a potent force for a change. Of course the Party was infiltrated by the secret police, and so too was the popular industrial movement for humane working conditions. At first the head of the Moscow *Okhrana* welcomed such economic action as a distraction from political agitation among the workers, and conducted a policy of 'police socialism' through *agents-provocateurs*. However, this tactic quickly ran out of control and in 1903 a rash of strikes brought out 250,000 workers. By this time, they had added a call for a general constituent assembly to their industrial demands. The authorities only regained the upper hand with difficulty, and that October the Imperial family took a welcome

break from the fervid atmosphere at home as guests at the 'wedding of the decade' – of their German niece Princess Alice of Battenberg, at Darmstadt. However, they returned to find domestic politics as troubled as ever.

In January 1904, the Tsar's chief minister observed to the Minister of war: 'What we need to hold Russia back from revolution is a small, victorious War.' Only days later the Japanese made a surprise attack on Russian warships in Port Arthur, a naval base on the Liaotang Peninsula between Korea and China. Trouble had been brewing on Russia's eastern frontier for years. Nicholas dreamed of a grand Imperial mission in Asia. In this he was actively encouraged by his German cousin, Kaiser William II, who entertained similar grandiose notions about the historic role of Christendom against the 'Yellow Peril'. Russian designs eventually focussed on the 'neutral' territories of Manchuria and Korea – which Japan reckoned to be within its own sphere of interest. Japan's chief advantage lay in the problems which the vast distances of Siberia presented to any concentration of Russian forces. Hence, sudden, surprise attack was indeed a sound military strategy. In no way dismayed,

the Russian Court looked forward to an easy victory over the Japanese, who they referred to as *'makaki'* ('little apes'). In fact, thanks to difficult logistics, Court interference and military incompetence, there followed an unrelieved series of Russian disasters. This, too, spurred the enemies of the regime at home.

When Port Arthur fell in January 1905, St Petersburg was wracked by industrial strife. On the first Sunday of that month a demonstration of thousands of men, women and children converged on the great square in front of the Winter Palace, bearing a petition to the Tsar. They were carrying sacred icons and pictures of the Tsar, and were singing the national anthem. As Nicholas and his family were at the Summer Palace of Tsarskoe Selo, on the out-

Top left, *the Tsar and Tsarina entertain President Faure of France, on a state visit.* Top right, *Nicholas among officers and troops on campaign; one of the few roles of monarchy he enjoyed playing.* Left, *a family photograph which contains many of the crowned heads of Europe. Besides Nicholas and Alexandra and their children, the picture includes: Queen Alexandra of Great Britain, King Frederick VIII of Denmark, King George I of the Hellenes and King Edward VII.*

skirts of the city, the marchers came cheerfully on through the snow. However, the Ministry of the Interior had prepared a welcome for them. By the end of 'Bloody Sunday', hundreds lay dead or wounded in the grey-red slush – shot down by the Tsar's troops. Henceforth, the 'little father' would be known as 'Nicholas the Bloody'.

Throughout 1905, terrorism and industrial action became more widespread. In June, the crew of the battleship *Potemkin* raised the Red Flag in an 11-day mutiny: in St Petersburg, even the *corps de ballet* at the Maryinsky Theatre refused to take the stage. Meanwhile, the whole of the Russian fleet was overwhelmed by the Japanese at Tsushima. Europe was stunned, and the Kaiser feared for the life of the Tsar in the revolution he supposed must follow. America feared for the altered balance of power in the Pacific. But in September – when President Theodore Roosevelt mediated at the Peace of Portsmouth, New Hampshire – Russia emerged surprisingly well despite Japan's overwhelming military victory. By this time though, the catalogue of defeat and brutal repression had entirely discredited the Tsar's regime at home.

Under great pressure, and at the insistence of his chief minister, Nicholas tried to contain the situation by granting political concessions in the so-called 'October Manifesto' of 1905. This promised an elected, representative assembly to be called the Duma. However, to ensure that this body would not present them with any problems, the Tsar's government framed the voting arrangements to guarantee a large number of peasant deputies – whose traditional loyalty could still be relied on. In order to remain financially independent of the new assembly they also secured a massive loan from France. Then, in April 1906, the Tsar promulgated new 'Fundamental Laws of the Empire' which not only reasserted the 'supreme autocratic power' of the Emperor, but also provided that only *he* could change them. Nicholas – who refused to even allow the word 'constitution' to be spoken in his hearing – had blocked the road to constitutional political change to his people.

The State opening of the Duma in April 1906 was stage-managed to overawe the delegates. A tableau of ministers and courtiers resplendent in uniforms and ceremonial dress, their wives with their halo-like *cacoshnics* and glittering with jewels, confronted the Deputies dressed in a motley ranging from formal evening-dress to peasant costumes and work clothes. However no one was overawed, and the Duma proved solid in opposition to the Tsar and his 'Fundamental Laws'. To his astonishment, after 10 years in power Nicholas could no longer even rely on the age-old loyalty of the peasantry. As a result, the assembly was shortly dissolved; but then the second Duma was still more hostile. Not until 1907 did the government's gerrymandering of the electoral process produce a sufficiently compliant, third Duma. Politically, it was an irrelevance.

In 1910, the Russian press had begun to carry reports of a Holy Man named 'Rasputin'. This 38-year-old from Siberia – Grigori Yefimovich – had in fact arrived in the capital some years before. With his coarse manners and powerful build, a long black beard and piercing eyes, he was undoubtedly a man of charismatic presence. He preached his own brand of occult sex and religiosity with hypnotic effect to a fashionable following, and soon came to the attention of the Empress.

Since the birth of her son Alexei in 1904, the Tsarina had lived with the dreadful knowledge that her baby suffered from haemophilia. This disease, which caused continual bleeding because of the blood's inability to clot, had been transmitted through the female side of the royal line from Victoria. So – unpopular, withdrawn from the Court and involved in her religious fantasies – the Tsarina welcomed Rasputin. Moreover, his presence did undoubtedly stop the boy's bleedings where the doctors were helpless. Before long Alexandra had come to regard this strange man as a 'divine messenger' . . . and the Tsar meekly shared her opinion.

Early in 1911, the talented minister Stolypin presented the Emperor with a report on Rasputin and demanded his banishment. This earned him the bitter enmity of the Empress, and in September of that year he was assassinated. Although he lingered for four days on his death bed, the Tsar made no move to visit him. There is now little doubt that the murder of Stolypin was contrived by the secret police.

The turbulent events that followed have become one of the momentous clichés of modern history, in which the fate of the Imperial family is generally classed as a romantic irrelevance. Yet the mystery surrounding their deaths is

Riots and demonstrations were a recurrent feature of the reign of Nicholas II. There were serious troubles in Moscow in 1901 (left). The Socialist Revolutionary Party was a spearhead of agitation for some years, with its own 'combat organization' for political assassination. Below, the imperial family arriving for the opening of the 1906 Duma.

one of the few things about modern Russia that can be guaranteed to stir popular interest in the West.

The day after the Tsar's abdication, a provisional government was cobbled together between the remaining members of the Duma and the revolutionary leaders of the Left. The royal family was hustled off into house-arrest in their rococo Summer Palace at Tsarskoe Selo (now re-named Gorky), a few miles south of St Petersburg – which had been re-named Petrograd in 1914 to remove any suggestion of German influence, and which would again be re-named as Leningrad in 1924. The press, in full cry, accused the Tsar of plotting with the Germans to regain his throne, and the leaders of the Petrograd Soviet – a soldiers' and workers' council that was to provide the model for revolutionary organizations throughout the country – demanded that he and his family be thrown into a common prison. However, the new minister of justice, Alexander Kerensky, refused their demands with the words: 'The Russian Revolution does not take vengeance.' Kerensky was soon to head the government, and during his short terms of office he

saw to it that his words held good – but the situation was precarious.

With the main resistance removed or frightened into compliance, Rasputin's associates soon took over the highest offices of government. Even reports of his debauches were discounted as malicious gossip by the Empress and ignored by the Tsar. By 1912, copies of the Empress's letters to Rasputin – written in terms little short of idolatry – were circulating in the capital, together with wild rumours that she and her daughters were part of his aristocratic harem. By this time, the danger to the dynasty was clear to everyone except the Tsar and Empress.

Despite all Russia's economic, social and political ills, the scandal of Rasputin's influence grew until it became – incredibly – the most serious threat to the Tsarist regime. But then the war clouds that had long been gathering in Europe suddenly diverted the Russian public's attention. At the end of July 1914 the government ordered full mobilization of its ill-prepared military forces in support of Serbia against Austria-Hungary. Then, two days later, Germany declared war on Russia.

Almost overnight, the country found itself united in patriotic fervour. A vast crowd assembled outside the Winter Palace to hear Nicholas – simply dressed in an infantry uniform – pledge the nation to the coming struggle. But pledges were not enough, and disillusionment followed swiftly as Russia lost 4,000,000 soldiers in 1915 and the High Command ordered a scorched-earth policy to slow German advances. Millions of Russian civilians were forced to leave their burning homesteads as refugees, and they trekked eastwards carrying what few possessions they could. As the nation disintegrated around him, Nicholas decided to take over the supreme command of the forces in the field.

From then on, Alexandra became the Tsar's deputy in the capital, and through her he transmitted his directives to his ministers. In return, however, he received scatterbrained advice – on which he often acted – which was largely dictated to the Tsarina by Rasputin. In fact, with her adored husband gone to 'write a glorious page in the history of Russia', Alexandra revelled in her new-found freedom to install ministers who had the approval of 'our friend' – the Man of God. And in this Ruritanian state of affairs Rasputin ordered changes of officials as rapidly as he changed his mistresses.

Finally, in the last weeks of December 1916, Rasputin was murdered in the St Petersburg palace of Prince Yusu-

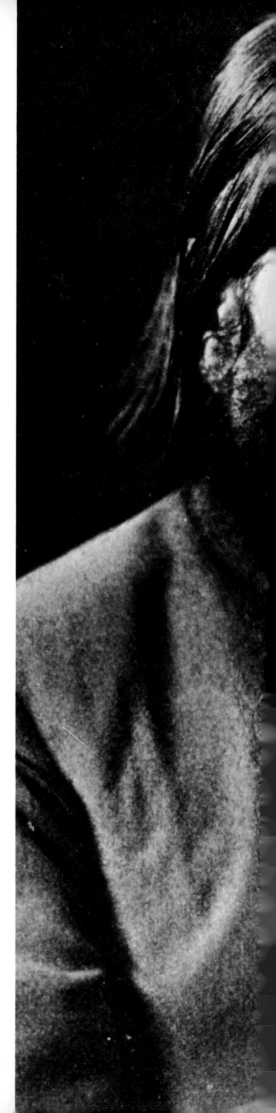

pov. But the deed had not been simply done. The young aristocratic assassins had first had to watch as a lethal dose of poison left the Mystic unaffected. Then they poured bullets into him, but still he struggled for life. Finally, they threw his dying body into the freezing waters of the Neva River. It was later dredged out on the orders of the Imperial family and privately interred.

Two months later, with the discredited dynasty largely forgotten, the capital broke out in an uproar of strikes, riots and army mutinies. As he tried to return to St Petersburg from the battle front, the Tsar found the railway tracks blocked by mutinous troops who diverted his train to Pskov. There, on the evening of 15 March 1917, he sat alone in his private railway compartment and signed his abdication. To the end he was indecisive. At first he intended to stand down in favour of his son, but then he changed his mind and nominated his brother Mikhail instead.

Far left, *the Tsar and his son, the most popular photograph of them ever taken.* Left, *Rasputin, the evil genius of the last years of Nicholas's reign.* Above, *Alexandra as a nurse in World War I.*

59

When the Grand Duke declined the position Russia's long centuries of autocracy were finally over.

At Tsarskoe Selo, the Tsar, Tsarina and their children had become fearful pawns in a waiting game. At first though, they easily enough adapted to the simple life imposed on them. With spring on the way they dug themselves a vegetable garden in the glorious grounds, and Nicholas himself chopped the wood for their household stove. In this eerie idyll under the watchful eyes of armed guards, there must have been harsh echoes of the happy childhood days spent playing at peasants in the model farms on the Imperial estates.

Meanwhile, in the real world outside, the hard men were moving to control events. Thanks to the courtesy of a sealed train provided by the German authorities, Lenin was back in Russia.

Germany's warlords had correctly calculated that the Bolsheviks under his leadership would prove far more valuable allies than a restored Nicholas. Whereas the Tsar still fondly hoped for a victory in the War, Lenin wanted peace on any terms in order to clear the way for what he and Trotsky planned to be the 'true revolution'. So, with the Treaty signed at Brest-Litovsk in December, Russia indeed got its peace . . . after signing away huge territorial concessions.

By then the Bolsheviks had been in control of Russia for three months, and the Imperial family's prospects were looking even more bleak. In August, faced by the growing power of Bolshevik agitation, Kerensky had sent them to Tobolsk in remote Siberia. But when the Bolsheviks came to power, the fairly mild regime of house-arrest immedi-

ately gave way to imprisonment. A stockade was built around the entrance to the house and the family were put on soldiers' rations. As the long months of the Siberian winter dragged wearily by, their guards became increasingly hostile. Rumour spoke of plots to release the family. So, in April 1918, they were moved again. This time the destination was Ekaterinburg in the Urals. Nicholas was uneasy: 'Judging from the local papers,' he commented, 'the workers there are bitterly hostile to me.'

On arrival, they were signed for on an itemized receipt by the executive of the local soviet. They were then ushered into their new place of confinement, Ipatiev House, with the words: 'Citizen Romanov, you may enter.' The Tsarina marked the date on the wall of her room with a good-luck sign. Besides some servants, only the Grand Duchess

Maria accompanied the Tsar and Tsarina. Their other children – Olga, Tatiana, Anastasia and Alexei – had stayed behind when Alexei suffered a severe crisis in his disease. However he soon recovered, and the family was reunited three weeks later.

As the weeks went by, the royal family sweltered in the heat of the Urals summer – but their windows were kept shut and were white-washed over as a security precaution. Alexei – 14 years old, with 'waxen face and eyes sad like an animal pursued by wolves' – was wracked by his fearful illness. As the guards diverted themselves with coarse innuendos at the expense of the young Grand Duchesses, the family shut in behind the walls of this 'House of Special Purpose' passed their days in dreadful apprehension. The only chance – though one they knew little of

– was the advance of a White Russian army which, by 14 July, seemed certain to take Ekaterinburg as its next objective in the civil war that was raging with the Reds.

According to the generally accepted version of the events that followed, the Imperial family were massacred by gunfire on the night of 15 July, and their bodies were burned. However, there is little evidence to support this – or any other – account, and so the mystery lives on. Between 1938 and 1970, a woman known to the world as Anna Anderson – but claiming to be the Grand Duchess Anastasia – persisted in litigation to prove that she was the surviving daughter of the Tsar. Then, in 1976, a book was published that made a persuasive case for the theory that Nicholas and his heir did indeed die at Ekaterinburg, but the women of the

family were smuggled away alive to Perm in the Urals, some 200 miles north-west of Ekaterinburg. However, this was just the latest in a long series of studies, among them secret Russian investigations, which have persistently questioned the official account of the Romanovs' fate. Nonetheless, 'Anastasia' remains the only person to claim she survived and escaped; neither the Tsarina, Olga or Tatiana ever re-appeared on the world stage.

In March 1917 the Tsar and his family were imprisoned in their summer palace at Tsarskoe Selo; thereafter conditions got worse. Above, the family on the roof of the house in which they were held at Tobolsk, in the Urals. Left, the house at Ipatief where the Tsar and probably the rest of the family were murdered.

News Chronicle

No. 31,057   FRIDAY, NOVEMBER 30, 1945   ONE PENNY

KING PETER DETHRONED, ACCUSES TITO

"I shall follow dictates of my conscience to liberate Yugo-Slavia"

TWENTY-TWO-YEAR-OLD King Peter II. of Yugo-Slavia, who was yesterday dethroned, issued this statement in London last night:

" I am fully conscious of my duties towards my country, and despite all steps taken against me by the present regime I shall continue to follow the clear dictates of my conscience to liberate Yugo-Slavia from tyranny—no matter whence it comes.

Revolutions and Kings

At 9 o'clock on the morning of 26 March 1941, the 18-year-old King Peter II of Yugoslavia switched on the radio in a drawing-room of the Marble Palace, Belgrade. Somewhat startled, he listened as 'the King' announced a *coup d'etat*. The voice – that of a young officer whom Peter later met – went on to assert that the Regency Council headed by Prince Paul, his uncle, had accepted the coup and asked General Simovic to form a new government.

About 6 AM on 26 March 1941 King Peter of Yugoslavia had been woken by his valet. Donning his clothes he had hurried down into the courtyard and piled into a staff car at the side of General Kosic. They drove at speed to the guards' barrack, where the bemused troops were drawn up in a special early-morning parade. The tottering government had decided that Peter should show himself to them in a last desperate attempt to ensure their loyalty. The radio soon told them how successful that particular ploy had been. By the end of the day, the King had discharged his first duties as 'acting monarch' by signing the papers authorizing the Simovic appointment and, incidentally, the declaration read in 'his voice' that morning.

Although that radio 'montage' introduced an unexpected touch of modernity to the proceedings, the hectic comings and goings of the coup were otherwise well fitted to the troubled traditions of Balkan politics. These traditions had their roots in numerous 19th-century liberation struggles against the long-standing domination of the Turkish Empire – struggles that had been confused throughout by interventions from Russia and Austria–

Hungary, and by rivalries between the freedom-fighters themselves. In fact, Peter's own dynasty, the House of Karageorge, had been founded in the early 1880s by the peasant hero of Serbia, 'George the Black'. For the next 100 years its throne was contested by the descendants of George's former lieutenant, Obrenovich. Finally, in 1903, the last of the Obrenovich line – Alexander, and his wife Draga – were butchered in their palace during an army revolt which brought King Peter I Karageorge to the throne.

Before the Turkish conquests, medieval Serbia and Bulgaria had been proud empires. The Croats – in the northwest of modern Yugoslavia – looked back to their legendary Prince Tomislav; whereas the mountainous principality of Montenegro in the south had long kept its independence against the Turkish imperial power. During the 19th century the rulers of Montenegro sometimes dreamed of leading a united south Slav state. The last of them, Prince Nicholas, was a flamboyant highlander like his subjects – most of whom, according to a eulogizing biographer, he knew by name. He was a central figure in the royal diplomacy of southern Europe, thanks to the marriages of

his daughters. Two became the consorts of Russian grand dukes, one married the Karageorge King, Peter I of Serbia and another Victor Emmanuel – later King of Italy. When a visitor, flattering Nicholas as the modernizer of Montenegro, mildly regretted that it had no exports, he jovially replied, 'But you forget my daughters.'

Although Nicholas behaved at times like some hero from a folk epic, and even enjoyed dispensing justice to his subjects under a venerable oak tree, he nonetheless chafed at his humiliating status as a mere Prince. Accordingly, in 1900, he assumed the title of Royal Highness, but this self-promotion drew criticism from many of his subjects who accused him of despotism. As a result, Nicholas was forced to concede a more liberal constitution in 1905. But then – despite an assassination attempt – the ageing autocrat finally prolaimed himself King of Montenegro in 1910. However, this lofty title did not long survive the outbreak of the World War I, in which Montenegro – allied with Serbia – suffered in the disastrous campaigns of 1915. Nicholas was forced to sign a hurried armistice with Austria–Hungary and himself flee into exile. He died, on the French Riviera, in March 1921.

Meanwhile, the Austrian Archduke Francis Ferdinand had been shot and killed at Sarajevo – the capital of the Austro–Hungarian province of Bosnia–Hercegovina – in July 1914. The assassins were young Serbian nationalists acting on orders from the 'Black Hand' organization. Rumours even suggested that Alexander – who had been acting as Regent for his father, Peter I of Serbia, since 14 June – was privy to the plot. If so, he reaped a terrible reward. In the outcry which followed the killing, Austrian public opinion demanded humiliation of the Serbs. However, the personal sympathies of Tsar Nicholas II of Russia lay with the Slav kingdom . . . so the juggernaut of international diplomacy lurched doggedly towards war.

At first the Serbian army astonished the world and held its own. But it was soon driven back, and spent much of the war cowering with detachments of British and other Allied troops at Salonika. Alexander staunchly held his forces together during the long ordeal, and – thanks to his Allies – was able to

Previous pages, *King Peter II of Yugoslavia at his desk in exile.* Above left, *Alexander I Obrenovich, assassinated 1903.* Below far left, *Peter I of Serbia;* left centre, *Peter I, with General Rogues in February 1916;* left, *with Nicholas II of Russia.* Above, *Prince Nicholas and Princess Milena.*

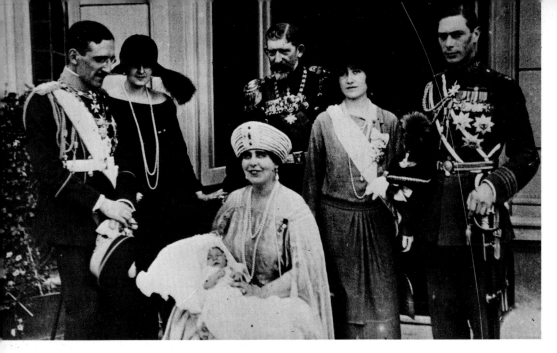

lead a victorious army back into Belgrade on 29 October 1918. The peace treaties that followed almost doubled the size of the war-torn Kingdom of Serbia – which gained Bosnia–Hercegovina (including Sarajevo itself), Dalmatia on the Adriatic coast, Croatia, Slovenia and parts of southern Hungary. In addition, the exiled Nicholas of Montenegro was finally voted off his throne by a national assembly which – faced with the occupation of the country by Serbian troops – opted to join the greater Serbia.

However, the fruits of Serbia's victory also held the seeds of discord. The regions were divided by religion – Catholicism, Eastern Orthodox and Islam; by language – Slovenian, Serbo–Croat and Hungarian; and even by alphabet – Cyrillic, Roman and Arab. Moreover, Croat nationalists – who had chafed under Austrian rule – boiled with anger at having to submit to their eastern, Slav neighbours. Old King Peter had once boasted: 'We Serbs are all peasants . . . my grandfather was a peasant and I set more store by that than by my throne.' Croats despised the Serbs for precisely these reasons – because they were all 'peasants' in their eyes. In reality, the lot of the true peasantry throughout the new Kingdom of the Serbs, Croats and Slovenes had scarcely improved since the days of Karageorge. The elections of 1919 – influenced as they were by the recent Russian Revolution – reflected the peasantry's restlessness by returning 58 Communists, the third-largest grouping in the Skupstina (parliament). However, that was to be the last free election in the country, and the last Skupstina to have Communist deputies until the coming of Tito.

The rivalries of the nationalities were not so easily dealt with. When Alexander came to the throne on his father's death in March 1921, he tactfully refused a coronation on the grounds of expense. In fact, in a country with three rival faiths, any religious rite would have been a symbol of division rather than unity. But Alexander did not mean to be a mere president, fearing that such a concession to republicans would open the way to a Soviet-style revolution. So, in 1921, he signed a new constitution which included drastic measures 'for the defence of the state'.

The King of the Serbs, Croats and Slovenes should have been *the* figurehead to inspire national loyalty, and elsewhere this has been the classic role of modern monarchy. Yet, in the arena of rival south Slav nationalisms, the Serbian royal house was unfitted for this role almost by definition. At first, Alexander's chief ministers were Serbs, and the Croat party led by Stephen Radic was in bitter opposition. Then, in 1925, Radic reversed his position, took office, became a regular visitor at Court and a particular favourite of Queen Marie. Then, in June 1928, he and four colleagues were shot down in the chamber of the Skupstina by a Montenegrin deputy. The Croat deputies immediately left Belgrade for Zagreb, and Alexander's aim to arbitrate between the contenders seemed doomed.

Alexander was, in any case, a somewhat aloof ruler. Whereas his father had cheerfully fought in the trenches side-by-side with his soldiers, Alexander began his personal reign by building a new royal palace in the hills outside Belgrade. The bustle of life in the capital irritated him, as did the people drinking at the sidewalk cafe tables beneath the palace windows and the unofficial delegations that queued outside the gates. Significantly, he chose Bled in faraway Slovenia as the site of his summer palace. He used the place as a reclusive retreat, while publicly proclaiming that his intention was to bring the monarch into contact with another of the Kingdom's regions.

Bled was also something of a centre of English life and culture. The King's cousin, Prince Paul, took a villa by Lake Bohinja some 12 miles away, and his relations – Prince Nicholas, Princess Helena of Greece and their daughter Princess Marina, later Duchess of Kent – were frequent house-guests. Prince Paul's children had an English governess, the household generally conversed in English, and the language was also used when visiting.

In 1922, Alexander married Marie, daughter of King Ferdinand and Queen Marie of Romania, and a granddaughter of Queen Victoria. 'Mignon', as she was known, nostalgically maintained her English sympathies. Their son Peter, the Crown Prince, was duly educated in England, and the Queen spoke the language whenever possible. Peter's birth assured the Queen's popularity in Serbia, where – in the more backward areas – a woman's primary

duty was still considered to be the bearing of sons. However, the Queen had no share in her husband's work.

Alexander, conscious no doubt of the prominent place occupied by Mignon's mother in the counsels of Ferdinand of Romania, made this clear when he announced: 'The Queen has no part in the affairs of state. I admire her because she is devoted to her children and seeks no other sphere of interest.' The Crown Prince was to retain awed memories of his serious, aloof father.

Then, in June 1928, the assassination of the Croat deputies shattered the façade of parliamentary cooperation. The following January, Alexander suspended the constitution to establish a personal dictatorship which was 'to improve the administration, eliminate corruption and bring about national unity'. Although Alexander's intentions were well-meant, the second point angered vested interests and the third once again stirred nationalist agitation. This was inflamed still further from the Serbian point of view when the King honoured the Catholic archbishop of Zagreb with the Serbian Order of Karageorge.

The country was renamed the 'Kingdom of Yugoslavia' ('of the south Slavs') on 3 October 1929. Its historic regions were renamed as administrative provinces, and even the national flag of Serbia was relegated to a museum. Yet the carefully controlled elections of

---

Above left, *the christening of Serbian Prince Peter, October 1923. King Alexander, Queen Elisabeth of Greece, Ferdinand of Romania and the Duke and duchess of York, surround Queen Marie of Romania, the child's grandmother. On 9 October 1934, Alexander of Yugoslavia landed at Marseilles for talks with French foreign minister Louis Barthould. Alexander and Barthould were assassinated by a Croat nationalist, Petrus Kalermen. Above, the King's chauffeur seizes Kalermen, later lynched by the crowd, while a trooper draws his sabre. Right, Reuter's dispatch.*

1931 still returned mostly Serb deputies . . . and all were supporters of the government. In response, Croat and Macedonian exiles and Communist underground groups fostered subversion, while Mussolini's Italy actively encouraged revolutionary action in neighbouring Croatia and Dalmatia.

Beset by domestic troubles and Italian intrigue, Alexander and his government nevertheless seemed to be moving towards rapprochement with Bulgaria – the old enemy. Macedonia, south of Serbia and bordering Greece and Bulgaria, was the region in dispute. It had been made over to Bulgaria at the Treaty of San Stefano between Russia and Turkey in 1878. Two years before that, Russia had forced the ailing Ottoman Empire to yield a measure of independence to Bulgaria under its own Prince, Alexander of Battenberg – a favourite nephew of the Tsar. From then on, Russia regarded this re-created Bulgaria – which was almost as large as the great medieval Bulgar Empire – as a major new field of influence. Of course Western European statesmen were dismayed, and within months they forced Russia to agree to a redrawing of the boundaries. The ensuing Treaty of Berlin, which Britain's Prime Minister Disraeli boasted was a 'peace with honour' thus saved a replay of the Crimean War. In the process, however, it also stripped Bulgaria of Macedonia. Today, a century later, many Bulgarians still hope for its recovery.

In 1885, Prince Alexander of Battenberg was succeeded by another German prince, Ferdinand of Coburg. Despite international ostracism and the opposition of Russia and Turkey, his vast personal fortune enabled him to improve the primitive amenities of Sofia and to maintain himself in some style. Nonetheless, when he visited Victoria at Balmoral he was received as Prince Ferdinand of Coburg, not as Prince of Bulgaria. At home he followed his nose – 'permanent like a cathedral', as Princess Pauline Metternich described it – through the thickets of domestic politics. He was indeed a wily Prince, and when the dictatorial chief minister Stambulow was assassinated in 1894, many assumed that he had had a hand in the matter.

At last, in 1896, Ferdinand won Russian recognition for his Crown – but the price was the confirmation of his two-year-old heir, Boris, in the Eastern Orthodox Church. Unfortunately, the boy had already been christened a Catholic, and Pope Leo XIII excommunicated his father for forcing his change of faith. As for Ferdinand's Queen, Princess Marie of Bourbon Parma – she left

Court with their younger son Kyril. Nonetheless, Ferdinand followed his ambition undeterred and in 1908 took advantage of revolution in Turkey to declare Bulgaria fully independent and himself 'Tsar' . . . the proud title of medieval Bulgaria's rulers.

In 1912, Ferdinand's next opportunist move was to join Serbia and Greece in a war which drove the Turks from much of their remaining European Empire. Although the Allies had agreed a division of Macedonia before the campaign, Ferdinand had dreams of conquering Constantinople – once capital of the Eastern Roman Christian Empire – and having himself crowned Emperor. Instead, when he found that his Allies had occupied Macedonia, he impetuously turned his armies on them. With the aid of Romania – which entered the war in July 1913 – Serbia and Greece soon forced a humiliating peace on Bulgaria. The dreams of Empire dissolved in talk of abdication. But to the embarrassment of gossipmongers in Karlsbad and other fashionable European resorts, 'Foxy' Ferdinand survived to fight again – in fact to share the defeat of Germany in World War I. And this time he *had* to go. In October 1918, the Bulgarian royal train – more luxurious even than that of the late Russian Tsar – steamed out of Sofia carrying the fallen monarch and his younger son Kyril into exile.

His children had always referred to Ferdinand as 'the monarch', even among themselves. It was no affectionate nickname. The man's despotic character was given full reign against them, against his courtiers, his servants and even his mistresses. His obsession with protocol made the Court a minefield. He collected superstitions, was plagued by phobias, haunted by premonitions and a devotee of the occult. No doubt he supposed that his concern for their health endeared him to his courtiers. As a hypochondriac, he always carried a tin filled with pills, pastilles and powders in colour-coded papers which 'he offered with a solicitous gesture to those who enjoyed the royal favour'. With more cause, he also kept ceaseless watch for conspiracies – often inviting visitors to inspect a basket piled high with denunciations of would-be assassins.

Ferdinand of Bulgaria, in his private life, was a well-known botanist and entomologist. He dreamed of recapturing Constantinople for Christianity and the fanciful painting (top left), The Emperor of the East, *hung for a time in Sofia cathedral.*

From the outset the new Tsar, 24-year-old Boris III, was more popular than his father had ever been. Not only did he speak fluent Bulgarian and bear the name of the great Tsars of the past, but he also stepped very carefully at first. He seemed to collaborate so readily with even the most radical measures of land reform proposed by the peasant party leader Stambolisky, that the burly politician was moved to declare jovially: 'If we make the republic we must keep Boris, for he would be the best of presidents.' Regrettably, when Stambolisky was assassinated in June 1923, some chose to suspect the monarch of complicity.

Certainly Boris was a shrewd and calculating young man, as he showed in 1919 when defeated Bulgaria was invaded by commissions from the victorious Allies. Like bailiffs, the commissions had come to assess the value of Bulgaria's assets, in order to extract heavy reparation payments for the costs of the War. However, Boris turned his considerable personal charm on the experts – held special audiences for journalists, and was successful in curbing the zeal with which the victors collected their dues. Moreover, his exiled father found his assets in England suddenly confiscated to help pay reparations.

On another occasion, stopping over in Paris on his return from King George V of England's coronation in 1910, the lively 17-year-old Crown Prince had had great fun evading his security guards by diving down into the Metro. Like his brothers and sisters, he thought of the royal palace as 'the prison'. Even so, his father's royal peculiarities had given him an enviable advantage over most other boys. For one thing, he actually learned to be an engine driver. Later, when he travelled his country as Tsar, crowds flocked to see their grimy monarch waving from the footplate.

Despite his own easy-going image, this 'popular' monarch in fact presided over a repressive, rightist regime which merely encouraged the cause of republican and communist agitators. Consequently, on 14 April 1925, as the royal car drove through the mountainous defile of Araba-Konak, a particularly determined attempt was made on the Tsar's life. In the first hail of bullets his passenger was killed and his chauffeur badly wounded. Seizing the steering wheel, Boris ground the gears into reverse and backed off quickly down the narrow, dusty road. Then, when the car

rode up the support cable of a telegraph post, he flung himself into the roadside ditch and scrambled on. Round the bend a local post-office bus came into view. As the King ran onto the road there was another burst of fire, but while the driver and passengers dashed for cover, the King drove the bus on to the nearest township. There, he ordered the telephone lines to Sofia to be cut and hurried on to reach the capital before news of the attempt. His coolness undoubtedly saved his own life, but it also dislocated the revolutionaries' plans and probably prevented bloody reprisals by the regime.

Then a second attack followed a few days later. On this occasion a distinguished congregation had assembled in the cathedral of St Nedelia in Sofia, for the funeral of a victim of the terror. As they waited for the royal party to arrive, a huge explosion shook the edifice. The massive cupola crashed down onto the crowded dignitaries and some 200 people were crushed to death under the broken masonry. This time not even the Tsar could hush-up the horror, and so the regime itself launched a reign of terror. Dimitrov, the leading Bulgarian communist, managed to flee into exile in Russia, but thousands of others were

much less fortunate than he was.

The following year the King travelled incognito to Western Europe, holidaying in the smart Swiss resorts, visiting his father at Coburg, and moving from place to place in continuing fear for his own life from revenge killers. He declined an offer to stay at a friend's mansion in Montreux with the comment: 'There is a memorial to the Empress Elisabeth there, I would rather stay at Lucerne which has not royal cenotaphs.' Like his father, Boris had a strong feeling for the powers of the occult. He had also inherited something of his father's obsession with health; but whereas Ferdinand offered quack remedies and superstitious nostrums, Boris followed the fashionable 'scientific' gurus beloved of smart society.

From 1927, Boris began to make frequent, regular visits to the West. Finally, in 1930 – after discreet enquiries around the salons of still-royal Europe by his brother Kyril and his sister – he married Giovanna, daughter of Victor Emmanuel III, the royal colleague of Mussolini. Yet when Boris later met the exiled King George II of Greece in London, he advised him not to link himself too closely with any dictator ... since 'dictators fall sooner or later and bring down those associated

with them'. This advice was all the more perplexing as Boris was changing his governments at will by the mid-1930s, and in 1938 he became his own, royal dictator.

Despite all this, Boris claimed to admire the conventional virtues of the constitutional monarchs. He visited Albert I ('the Good') of Belgium and, in 1933, was the guest of Britain's King George V at Balmoral. Unexpectedly, it was this amiable, old-fashioned gentleman who suggested a possible way to re-open communications with Yugoslavia without the danger of a rebuff. Since the 1890s Macedonia had been terrorized by freedom fighters who virtually ruled the small fraction of the region still on the Bulgarian side of the frontier. Boris wanted discrete negotiations.

Following King George's suggestion, he proposed to Alexander of Yugoslavia

Above left, *Queen Giovanna and Boris III of Bulgaria with token common children.* Above right, *Boris speaking to peasants after an earthquake.* Left, *the careworn Queen after her husband's death.*

71

a personal meeting in a suite at Belgrade railway station, during the stop of the Orient Express on its way to Sofia. Nowadays, airport meetings between ministers and Heads of State as they importantly hasten on their way from capital to capital are not unusual. In the 1930s, however, King George's idea was less familiar ... but it worked. Alexander, reluctant about the encounter, was warmed when Queen Giovanna embraced him at the unofficial welcome with the words, 'What a joy to meet you again, Sandro.' Her affection struck exactly the right note of family informality – which was of course the camouflage for this meeting of Heads of State. Friendship between kings does not change government policies, but later that year King Alexander received a stirring welcome when he visited Sofia. It seemed to herald a growing friendship between the two countries.

Romania, which did not receive its first King until 1881, became a communist republic in 1947. Yet during its brief epoch, the Romanian monarchy featured two of the most colourful royal figures of the 20th century. King Carol II was one of the shooting stars of European politics and high society between the wars; his mother, Queen Marie, startled the plenipotentiaries at the 1919 Peace Treaty of Versailles and later dazzled America.

During the Middle Ages, the territory of modern Romania – reaching north from the Danube towards Russia, and east to the Black Sea – was occupied by the Principalities of Moldavia and Wallachia. Early in the 15th century it was over-run by the Turks, who ousted the infamous Wallachian Prince Vlad 'the Impaler' (1462–75) – the real-life inspiration for the Dracula myth – and re-

mained as the suzerain power until 1881. However, from the 18th century the Romanov dynasty of Imperial Russia intervened increasingly in the area. In 1812 they forced the Turks to cede Bessarabia, but nine years later the 'Romanians' joined forces with their Turkish overlords to repel a Russian invasion. In return, the Ottoman authorities accepted native-born princes in place of Imperial governors.

Although these princes soon became agents of Russian imperialism, its cause suffered heavily from the setback of the Crimean War (1854–6). As a result, Russia had to return Bessarabia, and was forced to concur as the British and French formally guaranteed the Principalities' position within the Turkish Empire. With this guarantee behind them, Wallachia and Moldavia proclaimed themselves as the 'United Principality of Romania' in 1861. Five years later they elected Prince Karl Eitel of Hohenzollern–Sigmaringen – who was related to the Prussian royal family – as their ruler, and he was duly invested by the Sultan.

Then, in 1877, Romania allied itself with Russia in a war against Turkey. At the Congress of Berlin in the following year, Romania received full independence but had, once more, to return Bessarabia to Russia. However, when Tsar Alexander II was assassinated in March 1881, Russia accused the liberal Romanian government of harbouring republican sympathies. Within weeks – to placate their dangerous neighbours – Romania's politicians declared that Prince Carol (as he was known) would be their new King – Carol I. Established by a referendum, invested by a Turk, crowned by administrative decree, Carol's career from Prince to King of

Romania had indeed been chequered.

Although King Carol soon recognized Romania's need to industrialize, and began to exploit its oil resources, he ignored altogether the urgent matter of land reform. By 1907, the social discontent this caused had erupted into a short-lived revolution which was cruelly suppressed. During his reign, the Romanian government's foreign policy was influenced by Carol's German sympathies and his personal friendship with the Austrian Emperor Francis Joseph.

However, after his death in 1914, all that was to change. Carol was succeeded by his nephew Ferdinand, but many people thought that the new Queen – the beautiful and strong-willed Marie – was the power behind the throne. The daughter of Alfred, Duke of Edinburgh and Saxe–Coburg–Gotha, Marie had been born in 1875 in England, at Eastwell Park in Kent. As her father was the Commander of the British Mediterranean Fleet, she spent much of her childhood in the Commander's Residence in Malta. Then, when Duke Alfred acceded to the throne of Saxe–Coburg–Gotha, the family moved to the Castle of Coburg. Marie's betrothal to Prince Ferdinand was formally announced in Buckingham Palace; the marriage took place in the Castle of Sigmaringen, the family seat of her husband's family of Hohenzollern–Sigmaringen.

As Queen of Romania, Marie was immediately courted by the rival diplomats of Russia and Austria, and one Austrian minister flatteringly confided that she 'held the fate of her country in her hands'. A grand-daughter of Queen Victoria, Marie had chafed under the pro-German policies of the previous

reign, so Romania's declaration of war against the Central Powers in August 1916 may well have owed something to her influence. However, the army was in rout within weeks, Romania withdrew from the war, and the King and government were forced to flee Bucharest for the safety of Jassy, near the Russian border.

From there, the Queen plunged herself into Red Cross nursing. Day and night, she shirked neither the squalor nor the danger of primitive wartime hospitals. In her spare moments she plagued her royal relations Tsar Nicholas II of Russia and George V of England with letters detailing immense territorial claims for Romania in any post-war settlement. 'I knew,' she wrote later, 'that European geography had not been George's strong point, and I could almost see his wrinkled brow while labouring through my letter.' Nicholas, on the other hand, was not at all puzzled by the geography ... he was simply nonplussed by the claims.

Then, with the Revolution which swept Nicholas from his throne in 1917, the collapse of Russian power began. By November 1918, the Central Powers too were plunging to defeat. Tactfully, Romania re-opened hostilities against them on November 10 – one day before

Above left, *King Carol I of Romania.* Above centre, *Carol with Tsar Nicholas II.* Above right, *Sigmaringen, on the upper Danube, West Germany, the birthplace of Carol I and Ferdinand of Romania.* Left, *delayed by war, the coronation of Ferdinand and Marie of Romania was in October 1922. It was held at Alba Iulia, capital (1599–1601) of Walachia and Moldavia.*

73

the Armistice – and Ferdinand's 'Victorious' armies were able to annex Bessarabia from weakened Russia and sizeable territories from both Austria and Hungary. On 1 December, he and his Queen entered Bucharest in triumph, and the date is still celebrated as the anniversary of Romania's 'Reunification'.

Romania's opportunistic conquests were later recognized at the Versailles Peace Conference, with the Queen herself keeping a watchful eye on the proceedings from a 20-room suite in the Ritz. Of course her presence in Paris delighted the gossip columnists. As the only woman of standing to attend, she was there, she said, 'to give Romania a face in the affairs of the nations.' Her wardrobe – her principal diplomatic equipment – contained 60 gowns, 31 coats, 22 fur pieces, 29 hats and 83 pairs of dress slippers. 'I feel,' she observed, 'that this is not time for economies. Romania simply must have these territories, and what if for the lack of a gown a concession should be lost.' At home, Marie was known as 'the luck of the country'; though her practical influence on the negotiations may have

been less than she and her admirers liked to believe, Romania undoubtedly emerged in a fortunate position when the Peace Treaties were finally drawn up.

By this time, Queen Marie had become an international personality, and in 1926 she carried off a triumphant tour of the United States. But the happy days were drawing to a close. Ferdinand died in 1927, and the Queen's role in Romanian affairs was soon lost in the dramatic reign of her son, Carol II. She died in retirement in 1938.

Thirty-four at his father's death, Carol had already been keeping the gossips busy for some time. His youthful escapades had culminated in a morganatic marriage with one Mme Zizi Labrino, whom he then divorced to marry the long-suffering Princess Helen of Greece. However, theirs soon began to look like a marriage of royal convenience, as – shortly after the birth of Michael, his heir – Carol went off once again in pursuit of women. But when the news broke of his liaison with Mme Elena 'Magda' Lupescu, more than moral sensibilities were outraged.

Magda was of Jewish background, and in traditionally anti-semitic Romania that was something for which even a Prince's mistress could not be forgiven. So, in 1925, Carol was forced to renounce his right to the succession, and he and Magda went to live in Paris. On the death of Ferdinand, Carol's six-year-old son became King under a Regency. But then Carol returned in 1930, set his son aside, and had himself proclaimed king *de jure* since 1927. In the meantime, Queen Helen had been divorced in 1928, and so the King's beautiful red-haired mistress was proudly installed at the palace.

Although the Court Party was widely

unpopular throughout the country, its political opponents were at first divided. And then fascist, anti-semitic elements – in communication with the terrorist 'Iron Guard' (from 1933, the 'All-for-Fatherland Party') – became increasingly powerful until, in 1938, King Carol assumed personal dictatorial powers. He promptly proclaimed a corporate, syndicalist type of constitution, stage-managed a 'plebiscite', and had the leaders of the Iron Guard shot . . . 'while trying to escape'. But the playboy dictator did not last. Romania was weak abroad and lost territory to Russian, Bulgarian and Hungarian demands. In 1940, Carol was deposed by rightist elements in favour of his son.

Seven years later, Michael too was driven into exile as a communist regime was established in Romania. In the same year his wayward father at last married Magda, who appeared to be in the throes of a fatal illness. Later, when she recovered, the couple left their home in Brazil for Estoril in Portugal. There they formed part of a fashionable coterie of ex-royals including King Umberto of Italy, the Count of Paris and the Count of Barcelona. Carol died there in 1953.

Left, *Elisabeth of Wied (1843–1916), the popular queen of Carol I of Romania. Devoted to her people, she was also known throughout Europe for her books under the pen-name of Carmen Sylva.* Above left, *Ferdinand and Marie of Romania on their 1924 visit to England, arrive at Dover; they were welcomed by Edward, Prince of Wales.* Above right, *Marie of Romania with her children, at left Prince Carol.* Right, *Carol II of Romania at the 1926 Paris Automobile Salon.*

Spanish Succession

The accession of King Juan Carlos I in November 1975 marked the restoration of the Spanish monarchy after a lapse of 44 years. The political problems of modern Spain – compounded by demands for regional devolution in Catalonia and Valencia, and the terrorist violence of the Basque separatist movements – promise him a troubled reign. If so, that will be quite in keeping with the traditions of both his House and his country.

Back in 1808, Napoleon deposed Ferdinand VII to give his brother Joseph Bonaparte the throne. The Spanish Crown Jewels thus joined the hoard of loot Napoleon plundered from the rest of Europe – though according to one legend they are still walled up in a forgotten hiding place in the royal palace. Meanwhile, Ferdinand – held prisoner in Paris – became the mascot of the liberal idealists in Spain, but when he was restored he proved a ruthless and dull-witted reactionary. Rebellions in South America ended Spain's Empire there, while at home foreign troops kept Ferdinand on his throne.

His death opened another chapter of troubles. Since 1713, women had been excluded from the Spanish succession, but Ferdinand was persuaded by his young wife Maria Christina to change the law so that their baby daughter Isabella became heiress to the Crown. The King's brother, Don Carlos, was incensed. When Ferdinand died in 1833, and Isabella – just three years old – succeeded, the Carlists promptly embarked on civil war. The Regency government, headed by the Queen Mother, was supported by the progressives. The Pretender's support, on the other hand, came from reactionary political elements and also Basque and Catalan separatists hoping for concessions once they had their candidate on the throne. At last, in 1839, the government general, Baldomero Espartero, forced the Carlists to terms. He made himself Regent, was in turn overthrown in 1843, and Isabella – aged 13 – was declared Queen Regent. For the next 25 years, Spanish politics was a story of continuous Cabinet changes, repeated rebellions, and periods of dictatorship with the Catalans and Basques contributing their nationalist ambitions to the turmoil. Eventually, the hapless Queen was forced into exile in 1868.

In the next five years, Spain witnessed: a three-year 'constitutional monarchy' inaugurated by the Cortes (parliament) under the Italian-born King Amadeus; a 12-month republic; and two Carlist uprisings. By 1873, the Carlist cause seemed to have been suppressed in Catalonia and the Basque provinces. Two years later, Isabella's son – Alfonso XII – entered Madrid in triumph. He was 18, educated in Austria and England, clear-headed and generally popular. In the decade that followed, the monarchy was gradually consolidated. But the King died young in 1886, leaving a daughter and a pregnant Queen, Maria Christina. Meanwhile, the third Carlist, Don Carlos Duke of Madrid, was living in exile. But his cause was still very much alive, and

the Court awaited the birth of the royal child with agonized suspense.

As the Queen went into labour, the ante-rooms of the palace filled with tense courtiers, the ladies making their prayers for a male heir. As expectation reached its peak, 'the white and gold door of the Queen's chamber was opened. Between the sombre damask hangings the Prime Minister appeared. "King Alfonso XIII is born," he announced in a voice quivering with emotion.' A little later, the new-born baby 'was carried into the salon on a silver salver in awed silence, to receive the homage of the nobility and the diplomatic corps.' The last time a baby had been born a King was in 1316, when John I 'Posthumous' of France was born in

succession to his dead father, King Louis x. However, John I only lived for five days. In contrast, Alfonso XIII was destined to live and reign, and years later – in a classic remark – observed: 'I would like to know what heirs apparent think of their positions.'

The boy King received a largely military education, and was to follow military matters with close interest throughout his life. He assumed full regal powers on his 16th birthday in 1902. From exile in Italy, the Duke of Madrid issued a protest and assertion of his own rights. However, his attempt to enter Spain was foiled by French police at Perpignan, who politely but firmly requested that he turn back. Alfonso's induction and oath-taking was on 17 May, and 'all that the most magnificent pomp of monarchical luxury could display under the sun of Castile was lavished on the spectacle'. Meanwhile, the ancient flag of the Kingdom of Aragon fluttered under the sun of Barcelona.

Although Carlism still enjoyed sturdy support in some Catalan and Basque circles, the movement had by this time split into rival factions and was a spent force as a real threat. However, the handsome young King had inherited other problems from the ill-managed Regency of his mother. In January, a nervous censor had considered the monarchy's standing so insecure that he had blue-pencilled the *Marseillaise* from the score of an historical opera being performed at the Lisbon opera house. Nonetheless, the vivacious determination of the young King to meet his people earned him early popularity. On many occasions he managed to evade his security guards to make expeditions by car or on foot all over Madrid and its *environs*. Perhaps a little sourly, one Spaniard observed that the King was 'not content to occupy the throne, but must also

occupy Spain'. Once, during a tour of the north-west provinces, he and his entourage ignored the ministers in the official party in order to let the people at large catch sight of their monarch. The ministers did not take the snub kindly. Soon, others began to grumble about the royal preference for courtiers rather than constitutionally elected advisers.

Despite the animosity of conservatives that he provoked, Alfonso was conventionally right-wing in his politics, and once even refused to confer the new Order of Alfonso XIII on the author of an anti-clerical play. But he did know how to make a generous public gesture. In a grand ceremony held in March 1905 to honour José Echegaray – a distinguished liberal politician, economist and Nobel laureate for literature – Alfonso publicly embraced Echegaray, although the great man's plays had recently adopted a distinctly satirical tone. Nonetheless, public gestures could not govern a country in which the politicians seemed incapable of devising a stable pattern of government, and in which ministries followed one another 'like figures in a magic lantern'.

In 1904, the Cortes witnessed scenes of astonishing disorder. To the anger of the Court the furious debates were not even suspended for the funeral of the King's sister, the Princess of the Asturias, who had died in childbirth that October. In fact that month ended with a storm of shouting that continued virtually uninterrupted from 3.00pm on Saturday the 29th to the morning of Monday the 31st – the President broke three bells in his vain attempts to bring the uproar to an end. Yet when Alfonso suspended the assembly in December, and installed the extreme rightist General Azcarraga as President of the Senate, even conservatives were dismayed. Over the next 20 years, as the mill race of Spanish politics tumbled on its course, the King intervened regularly, taking advice from politicians of his own choosing, whether ministers or not. However, his interventions had little discernible effect except, possibly, to make the pace more hectic.

Truces in the political dog-fight were

Previous pages, *King Alfonso XIII*. Far left, *the young Alfonso XIII of Spain*. Above, *the royal palace, Madrid*. Left, *Alfonso being sworn in as king, 1902. Spanish monarchs are not crowned but take an oath (the jura) to the constitution, in the palace of the Cortes in the presence of the assembled members of parliament.*

Far right, *the 20-year-old King Alfonso and his fiancée Princess Victoria Eugenie Battenberg, known as 'Ena'. In Protestant England, the Princess's home, there was opposition to this union with a Catholic family; reactionary Spaniards feared the King might fall prey to Freemasonry. In fact, the young couple were in greater danger from anarchists opposed to monarchy.* Above, *the scene shortly after the explosion of a bomb thrown at the marriage procession on 31 May 1906.*

sometimes arranged while Alfonso was out of the country on State Visits. In 1905 he was in Paris. On 1 June, as he and President Loubet were riding in their state carriage, a bomb was thrown by a Spanish anarchist – it was the first of a number of unsuccessful attempts on the King's life. However, in the following year he became the focus for political controversy in England, when news broke of his betrothal to Princess Victoria Eugenie ('Ena') Battenberg.

The idea of an English princess near to the royal family marrying a Catholic drew protests from the Church Association and the Protestant

Alliance. But King Edward VII refused all petitions to withold his consent and, as no vote of funds for her dowry was in prospect, the matter did not come up in Parliament. However, Spain's Catholic bigots were also perturbed. In the year of the betrothal, Alfonso's ministers had proposed legislation to give civil marriages between Spanish Catholics legal validity – forthwith the Archbishop of Valencia compared the King to the Emperor Diocletian, the ruthless Roman persecutor of the Christians. Moreover, only a few years before, another bishop had affirmed that the former Catholic Empire of

Spain had been lost through Freemason intrigue . . . and King Edward VII's sympathy for Freemasonry was well known. In such a country, it was hardly surprising that many viewed the English marrage with suspicion, even though the Princess had adopted the religion of her spouse.

The marriage, to the accompaniment of festivities that lasted a month, was solemnized on 31 May. As the royal procession returned from the church through streets full of cheering crowds, the scene suddenly exploded in screaming panic. A bomb thrown by an anarchist, Matteo Morales, had killed the horses of the royal carriage and spattered the bride's sun-dazzled dress with blood. Miraculously, the King and Queen were unhurt. Alfonso ran back down the procession reassuring his family and giving orders to his equerries to look after the injured spectators. A veteran of such hazards, he quipped: 'It's all a part of being King.' The young Queen paled, but kept her composure until she reached the privacy of her palace apartments. The next day she was able to take her place at a bullfight arranged in her honour.

The following year saw monarchist and separatist violence in the streets of Barcelona which was put down with government brutality. The Catalans, like the Basques, are heirs to proud and ancient traditions independent of the Castilian central government. Alfonso

recognized this indomitable historical spirit, and tried to temper government violence with conciliatory gestures. In March 1908, taking advantage of a visit by ships of the Austrian navy in Barcelona harbour, he made a State Progress there and moved through the crowded streets to enthusiastic cheers, without escort. In October he was once again in Barcelona, and he responded to the mayor's address of welcome in Catalan in the same language.

But such gestures of goodwill were no answer to the frustrated bitterness of the activists. In July 1909, a general strike in Barcelona broke out into revolutionary violence and arson. Army intervention was followed by a two-month government reign of terror which caused press outcry throughout liberal Europe. The same year, the King faced two other problems. The Duke of Madrid died in July and the Carlists immediately recognized his successor; while an incident in Spanish Morocco caused the King to abandon his round of polo games, motor tours and visits to fashionable aviators to make encouraging speeches to his troops. Two years later he visited military posts in North Africa itself.

However, 1911 was also marked by a much more unconventional royal initiative. Late in the year news reached Alfonso that his aunt – the Infanta Eulalia who lived in France – was planning to publish a book which, it

was rumoured, would be politically controversial. The King duly ordered the Princess to halt publication or lose her royal privileges. She declined ... and the King thought better of his threat. Nevertheless, Eulalia's English publishers seized the publicity potential and stamped 'The Book Forbidden by the King of Spain' all over the dust jacket. Years later an American congratulated the Infanta on what he supposed had been a sales operation contrived with the King's help to boost her takings. In fact, the political content of the book consisted of a few words mildly approving the ideals of socialism, but what had most probably started the rumour in the first place were Eulalia's feminist sentiments. They must certainly have startled many conventional Spanish ladies of the day, and indeed such views were unusual for any woman of her social rank at that time.

'... For centuries,' she wrote, 'man has denied woman her finest qualities which are fearlessness and presence of mind, and the majority of women have come to be convinced that these qualities are unwomanly and to be reckoned faults. ... Consider how sad was the lot of woman when, devoid of the means to free herself honestly from slavery she was compelled to sell herself, by legal marriage or otherwise.'

Aunt and nephew were reconciled; the Infanta's later books have nothing but praise for the King. In particular, she admired his work for prisoners and refugees during World War I. Like his government, Alfonso was determined to remain neutral, but he did not remain aloof. Under his direction Spanish embassies and consulates operated an information service for relatives of prisoners and refugees in the belligerent countries of Europe. In 1921, the King and Queen of the Belgians made a State Visit to Madrid and Barcelona to acknowledge their gratitude for all the work that has been done.

However, the year 1921 was clouded by news from Morocco. In July, after Spanish troops had been heavily defeated at Anual, a commission was set up. Over the next two years its investigations led it to conclude that the King's own interventions had played a large part in Spain's disastrous military record. Then, in September 1923 – just a week before the report was due for publication – a highly opportune military coup led by General Miguel Primo de Rivera overthrew the government. On September 15, the King appointed Primo de Rivera as president of a military directory. The Cabinet was dismissed, the ministries abolished, the Cortes dissolved and constitutional guarantees suspended. That November, the King and his dictator visited the Italy of Victor Emmanuel and Mussolini. The following June, the King and Queen of Italy returned the visit.

In 1925, the military directory was replaced by a civil dictatorship under Primo de Rivera. This oppressive regime was opposed by liberals, Catalan separatists, and many distinguished exiles such as the novelist Vicente Blasco Ibanez and the philosopher Miguel de Unamuno. Nonetheless, the 21 years before the *coup* had witnessed no fewer than 33 administrations, and many Spaniards must have welcomed the new stability even at the cost of dictatorship. On 25 January 1925, over 9,000 alcaldes and mayors marched in procession past the royal palace in Madrid to celebrate the King's name day. Yet, as the royal train returned in May from a visit to Catalonia, it was wrecked by terrorist action. The following year there were army mutinies in Segovia, Valladolid and Pamplona. With such crises afoot, the King left the beaches of San Sebastian for Madrid. However, after a few days the hastily imposed state of martial law could be lifted, and the King was then free to return to the seaside.

Throughout his troubled reign King Alfonso was a brilliant figure in the social life of Spain and Europe. He was a keen golfer, one of the first in his country, and – under the 'incognito' of 'the Duke of Toledo' – he was an active all-round sportsman. According to the gossips, Alfonso was also an active dancing partner to many beautiful women other than his wife at such fashionable resorts as Deauville on the north coast of France. Unfortunately, his strong-man dictator was not strong enough to take care of business at home. Despite ambitious plans for economic expansion, Spain still stumbled in the economic race. The late 20s were plagued with plots and rebellions which, although put down, constantly proclaimed the unrest of the country. Finally, in January 1930, the dictator resigned. Municipal elections the fol-

lowing year brought massive Republican gains, and on 4 April the King – having 'suspended the exercise of royal power' – went into exile.

Alfonso had long been a central figure on the Spanish political stage, and it was only fair in the circumstances that he should forfeit his position even if, stubbornly, he never formally abdicated. In fact he had enjoyed some popularity with his people. In exile, he could look back on 1914, when even some Republicans had acknowledged his patriotism and few of his subjects – as ever – had doubted his courage. His impetuous bravery on the polo field and the presence of mind with which he had foiled an assassination attempt by rearing up his horse to receive the bullets were, perhaps, conventional instances of royal daring. But on a visit to the impoverished western region of Las Urdes, he had also dared to shake the hand of one of its leper community. It was an unlooked-for and doubtless long-remembered gesture from the mercurial monarch.

In the spring of 1929, Lord Louis Mountbatten and his wife were passing

Above left, *King Alfonso with General Primo de Rivera at the time of the latter's coup in September 1913.* Above centre, *with Primo de Rivera and the Marquis of Viana on a shooting party during a tour of Jaén province.* Above right, *the royal family on holiday at the fashionable northern coastal resort of Santander.* Right, *the King in pensive mood.*

through Barcelona. The slim and self-possessed Lady Edwina was not deterred from the trip by the fact that she was expecting a baby, and was only mildly annoyed when she found herself in premature labour. Her attentive husband, however, wanted the best gynaecologist available, and naturally rang his cousin Ena, the Queen of Spain. The King took the call and was absolutely delighted at the news. 'I don't know any doctor in Barcelona,' he cheerfully assured the worried Mountbatten, 'but I'll send a regiment right around to guard dear Edwina.' The soldiers duly clattered round in full-dress uniform to lend a touch of colour to the birth of Pamela Mountbatten. Naturally, the King became her godfather.

In contrast the history of Alfonso's own family was less happy. His wife, a descendant of Queen Victoria, was a carrier of the bleeding disease, haemophilia. Their eldest and youngest sons both died comparatively young of minor injuries that could not be staunched. The King's second son, Jaime, renounced his claim to the succession, so that it was to his third son – Juan, Count of Barcelona – that Alfonso transferred the claim, shortly before his own death in 1941. By this time, however, General Francisco Franco – after overthrowing the Republican Government that had succeeded Alfonso – had been firmly in power for five years. A fascist dictator, Franco was determined to keep the country in his grip.

In 1947, Franco promulgated a Law of Succession which declared Spain a Kingdom and himself Regent pending the choice of a King. The dictator held undisputed power, but at the age of 55 he had no heir. With characteristic guile he anticipated future struggles for power between his ambitious ministers by removing the question of succession from the political arena. He conferred it upon the family of the 37-year-old Count of Barcelona, whose constitutional right could hardly be disputed by Spain's ruling class. However, he did not immediately acknowledge the claims of the Count himself, as such an acknowledgement could have been interpreted as presenting Spain with a more legitimate government than that of his own military regime. Instead, Franco retained control of the succession, and if the monarchists accepted him as arbiter of the country's future they tacitly conceded his right to rule it in the present.

The Count agreed that his sons should be educated in Spain. The elder, Juan Carlos, was to be allowed 'to serve his country in a way appropriate to his rank and station'. He received a largely

military education first in Madrid, with a personal tutor, then at the Spanish military, naval and aviation academies. By 1960, when he was 22, Juan Carlos held commissions in both the army and air force and, following a further meeting between his father and Franco, that year he was enrolled for a two-year course at Madrid University. It became increasingly apparent that he, and not his 47-year-old father, was being groomed for the succession. Between 1963 and 1968 he was attached to various government ministries, and in 1969 his title was changed from Prince of the Asturias (the traditional title of the heir) to Prince of Spain. Finally, in 1971, Juan Carlos was proclaimed the Caudillo's heir.

In the summer of 1960, 'Juanito' – as he is known to his family – attended the wedding of the Duke of Kent in England. Among the guests was Princess Sophia of Greece – daughter of King Paul and Queen Frederika, and great grand-daughter of the Kaiser. They married in May the following year. Their wedding in Athens, under a royal-blue sky, was a fairy-tale celebration of a love match. The Queen was educated at the Kürt Hahn school in Salem, and then trained and worked for

a time as a nurse. So, in the words of Princess Viktoria Luise, her grandmother: 'She could prepare herself in every way for the duties which would fall to her as a princess.'

The royal couple have three children: Elena, born 1963; Cristina, born 1965; and Felippe, born 1968 and the heir to the throne. Among the guests at the Prince's christening was the former Queen Victoria-Eugenie. For her it was a doubly happy day – being her first visit to Spain since fleeing the country with her husband in 1931. The cheers of the crowds were fitting if nostalgic tributes to the grand old lady who died in the following year. With the onset of General Franco's last illness in the autumn of 1975, Juan Carlos assumed the functions of Head of State. In his first speech to the nation he proposed himself as: 'Mediator, guardian of the constitution and spokesman of justice. ... Together we can achieve everything, if everyone gets a fair chance.'

The wedding of Juan Carlos of Spain and Princess Sophia of Greece in May 1961. Left, *the formal picture after the ceremony.* Above, *the state coach passing through cheering crowds.*

Royal High Society

With the crash of falling empires echoing ever more faintly as the 1920s advanced, the high-life spots of Europe became the haunts of princes, ex-monarchs and one-time pretenders who were quite relieved to no longer have the cares of government or the risks of revolution hanging over their heads.

Prince Andrew of Greece was summarily thrown out of his country for alleged military incompetence. He became cynical, and – in the words of the distinguished royal biographer, Robert Lacey – 'gravitated to Monte Carlo and the quietly upholstered life of a playboy of modest means'.

One of Andrew's neighbours on the popular Riviera coast was Prince Danilo, the son of ex-King Nicholas of Montenegro. Nicholas had left his country quite quickly during World War I, and found – when it was over – that his people would not have him back. He died in exile in March 1921. It is doubtful whether Danilo felt any particular ill-will towards his father's former subjects, and he certainly had no plans to recover his crown. Instead, he slid gracefully into his 50s, content to be surrounded by luxuries made possible – in large part – by the resources of a wealthy wife.

Imagine his dismay when he found he had been tracked down to his elegant

home by 'a deputation of stalwart mountaineers, bristling with weapons according to the fashion of their country, vowing impassioned devotion to the person they called King'. Danilo, either unnerved by his uncouth 'subjects' or merely displaying his innate good manners, accepted the rights and titles they thrust upon him. However, after a reign of merely six days, he abdicated in favour of a nephew.

Other deposed European royals were, of course, more tenacious of their rights. King Ludwig III of Bavaria – a model farmer and a pleasantly inoffensive figure – was, for one, genuinely astonished when socialist revolution ousted him and his family in 1918. At the time, even the socialist August Bebel remarked that he would have made an ideal president. However, nobody asked him . . . and he certainly would not have accepted such a 'democratic' appointment. Indeed, King Ludwig refused to abdicate, although he did formally absolve the Bavarian armed forces and civil service from their oaths of allegiance to him. In exile, both he and his son Prince Rupprecht 'let it be known' that they would accept legal restoration.

Ludwig really seems to have believed that such a possibility was on the cards, and there were high ideals behind his refusal to relinquish his royal claims. 'I could be a rich man,' he observed, 'for money would undoubtedly be given to me if I consented to abdicate. But the Crown is too lofty and holy to be sold. I will never abandon my rights. I have always done my best for the people. But I have been driven away, I do not know why.'

Clearly it was Ludwig's tragedy, and that of many another overthrown monarch, to never really understand why they had been 'driven away'. Nor, one may suppose in the case of Bavaria once the revolutionary act was over, did many of the King's former subjects understand either. True, the Bavarian monarchs had mostly been oddly eccentric or plain mad, but Ludwig was not of that number and had been barely more powerful than an average president. Nor was Bavaria – the Nazi's home ground – to be better governed in the 1920s without a King than it had been before with one. What Ludwig did not realize, because he had never been introduced to the real world, was that

getting him out of the way had largely been a matter of clearing the air . . .

Among the many exiled royals who predictably faced a sad decline in their standards of living was the Kaiser's daughter, Viktoria Luise. She made a home with her family in Gmunden, Austria, and was once heard to remark: 'Much of our royal style of living has disappeared.' In fact her husband, Ernest Augustus, former Duke of Brunswick, had to raise money by selling the Crown Jewels and many of the treasures of his noble family of Guelf. And yet the royal world did not entirely forget them. In 1947, after attending the wedding of Princess Elizabeth of Great Britain and Prince Philip, his daughter Queen Frederika of Greece flew over to Hanover with Princess Marina of Kent for a party at the little family castle outside the town. The plane was made available by King George VI, and the welcome – which made the trip so memorable – was provided by the people of Hanover. The whole population, it seemed, had turned out to wish her father 'happy birthday'. Despite the appalling condition of post-war Germany, most had even followed the

old custom and brought the ex-Duke a chicken, a goose or a hare.

In fact, countries that have lost their royalty are often still fascinated by the doings of kings and queens. For example, when she is in need of a little light relief, Queen Elizabeth II may turn to the French press reports of her activities and those of her family. In 1972, the newspaper *France Dimanche* analysed its file on the British royal family. The reports went back over 14 years, and in that time the French public received: 16 reports of the Queen's coming abdication; 73 reports of her divorce from Prince Philip; 17 reports of snubs she had supposedly delivered to 'minor' royalty such as Princess Grace of Monaco; and no fewer than 92 reports of her own pregnancy! The Queen, it is said, genuinely admires the creative imagination that goes into these reports. Their mass readership, on the other hand, reveals a deep feeling of popular nostalgia for a lost world.

To committed monarchists, however, royalty is much more than just a matter for entertaining gossip and nostalgia. Between the wars, for instance, an Austrian loyalist said 'With Otto von Habsburg as Holy Roman Emperor there will be no need to fear the menace of another, more hideous war.' Since the Habsburgs themselves had abandoned the title of Holy Roman Emperor in 1806, this was fantasy of a high order. Yet for years the republican government of Austria took such sentiments so seriously that it refused Dr Habsburg permission to enter the country.

Even royalty have sometimes to be wary of their more irrational supporters. As we have seen, when Queen Victoria died there were English Jacobites who acclaimed the 'true line' in the person of a Bavarian princess. Later, when the Bavarian throne itself had toppled in the 1920s, Princess Mary – the woman in question – had still to refuse a request from two English Jacobites for an audience, 'lest she should lay herself open to misinterpretation'. More recently, at the time of the Arab–Israeli War in 1967, British television interviewed a gentleman by the name of Lusignan. Although he was living in humble circumstances in West London, Lusignan could trace his ancestry back to the medieval French family which had once had a claim to the crown of the Christian 'Kingdom of Jerusalem'. 'My people need me,' he said, and announced his intention of travelling to the United Nations to address the General Assembly. Flights of fancy like these can bring welcome light relief to the sombre landscape of today's world affairs.

Nowadays, surviving royalty is generally anxious to present its members as 'ordinary folk' like the rest of us. However, this must be a difficult image to maintain for those born to a reality of royal power. On one famous occasion, for example, Queen Wilhelmina of the Netherlands – aged 10 and a strong-willed child – was absolutely delighted by enthusiastic demonstrations of loyalty from crowds outside the palace. When her nanny refused her pleas to stay up past her bedtime, Wilhelmina lost her patience and declared: 'If you send me to bed, I shall appeal to my people from the balcony.' However, the authoritative young Queen's ego may have been a little deflated during a visit to Victoria at Windsor Castle in 1895. After lunch, the indulgent old lady turned to her with the words, 'And what can we do to amuse you now, my child?'

Victoria loved children, and was never happier than when she was surrounded by young members of her for-ever growing family. Her stately daughter-in-law, the beautiful Alexandra of Denmark, also presided over a household bustling with happiness. Her son, the young Prince George, never forgot his happy days spent in the nursery. Years later, when he was King George V, his older sister Princess Victoria always started a telephone chat with: 'Is that you, my old fool?' Once, she found herself being answered by the palace operator who replied: 'No your Royal Highness, His Majesty is not yet on the line.'

As the 20th century progresses, more and more princes and kings-to-be are being educated in schools like 'ordinary folk' rather than by palace tutors. However, even the most sincere attempts to educate princes in a democratic style can be thwarted. For instance, when his father was assassinated, 11-year-old Peter of Yugoslavia found himself abruptly removed from his English school and driven to London to prepare himself for the journey home. Overnight, the schoolboy who had been happy to muck in with his friends in the classroom or at school camp suddenly found himself being saluted as King. He broke down in tears. 'Nobody can be King but Papa,' he protested in vain.

Previous pages, *Prince Rainier of Monaco and a view of Monte Carlo.* Above, *apartment in the Herrenchiemsee palace, Bavaria.* Left, *Prince Danilo of Montenegro (d. 1939) with his bride Militza. Danilo's nephew, Michael, was nominally king of Montenegro from 1921.*

Nonetheless, royal styles of education have certainly altered radically in recent times. A century ago, Humbert I of Italy was anxious that his heir, the Prince of Naples – later King Victor Emmanuel III – should have the best education available. Accordingly, the boy began his primary schooling traditionally enough under the watchful eye of a governess, one – inevitably English – Miss Elizabeth Lee. For his secondary education Victor Emmanuel was sent to public academies, but he received his lessons from the professors in the privacy of his own lodgings. At exam-time, though, he faced a truly royal ordeal. His exams were held in one of the gilded halls of the palace, in the presence of the King and Queen. Seated behind a long table were the minister of war, the head of the army staff, the first adjutant field-general and other worthies. Facing them, the Prince sat alone at a small writing desk. Each subject to be tested – from geography and languages to military tactics – was represented by a coloured ball. The examination started with the balls being placed in a bag by the minister of war. The Prince himself pulled out one of the balls, and the questioning began. The whole ceremony followed a programme tied up in ribbons of Italy's national colours. However, when Victor Emmanuel visited Windsor Castle in the 1880s, Queen Victoria voiced her magisterial approval of the end product, saying: 'The Prince of Naples is the most intelligent prince in Europe.' As she had met most of them Victoria was no doubt in a good position to judge.

In contrast, even Hitler occasionally tried to enlist the social circle of monarchy in his schemes. Although his approaches to Otto of Habsburg are well known, Hitler's attitude to the institution of royalty was a strange mixture of contempt and superstition. Otto Dietrich, his press chief, once recalled a meeting with Goebbels and other leaders during which the Führer dozed off. Waking with a start from his dreams, he turned to Goebbels and – to the latter's intense embarrassment – said in an urgent voice: 'You must on no account make me Kaiser or King.' Another, less surprising outburst, occurred during one of Hitler's rare visits to the opera at Dresden. On arriving, he

happened to notice a gold crown over the door of the box assigned to him, and was informed by the proud local officials that it had once been the box of the Kings of Saxony. Hearing this, the Führer screamed: 'And you expect me to sit in the box of an abdicated king? Never.' With that, he turned on his heel and stalked out of the theatre.

Behind the scenes, however, there is no doubt that Hitler regarded royalty as potentially useful recruits to his cause. In particular, he viewed the accession of Edward VIII of England with great interest, and once famously opined 'what a good Queen' Mrs Simpson would make. Long before that, however, he and Ribbentrop had already suggested to Viktoria Luise, the ex-Kaiser's daughter, that she should try to arrange the marriage of her daughter Frederike to Edward when he was Prince of Wales. However, Princess Viktoria had refused to countenance the idea that her family should form an unofficial diplomatic link between its English cousins and the Nazi regime.

Nonetheless, there are clear indications that Edward's own political sympathies were well to the Right. During one visit to Germany, for instance, he was not only warmly entertained by the Nazi leaders, but he also even essayed a hesitant raised-arm salute. In 1939, at the outbreak of World War II, he was attached in a liaison capacity to the British Expeditionary Force in France. When the French capitulated in 1940, he made his way to Lisbon and stayed for two weeks in the Portuguese capital. During that time he had discussions with German agents, who had been briefed by Ribbentrop to explore the possibility of him resuming the throne. Although the Duke would not contemplate any such schemes, the agents were able to report that he was 'convinced that if he had remained on the throne, war would have been avoided'.

Like many of his generation, Edward believed that nothing could warrant the return of war to Europe. Like many, he had joined the dance mania of the '20s in relief after the horrors of 1914–18. Perhaps he never fully grew out of the attitudes of that carefree, irresponsible decade. 'Peter Pan' – as some of his acquaintances called him – had his 'Never-Never Land' at Fort Belvedere, a pseudo-Gothic turreted house on the edge of Windsor Great Park. This became his retreat from the tedium of state functions and the glare of publicity. Visitors there might come upon him sawing down unwanted trees or clearing the undergrowth wearing a Guardsman's bearskin busby which was

Above, *King Umberto I of Italy.*
Centre, *his son King Victor Emmanuel III, in his early 30s.* Left, *Edward, Duke of Windsor, with Mrs Wallis Simpson, shortly after his abdication.*

being 'broken in for some state occasion'. Most guests found themselves pressed into service. One of his many female companions, the American Lady Thelma Furness, was a constant visitor at 'The Fort'. It was at her London house, in 1930, that the Prince first met Mr and Mrs Simpson – friends of Thelma's elder sister. Before long, the Prince's attachment to Mrs. Simpson – a divorcee – would expose him, as King, to the pressure of harsh, mundane realities that must have seemed far distant from his dreamy privileged existence as the 'Playboy Prince'. The choice he eventually had to make, and the build-up to its inevitably sad outcome, are dealt with in the following chapter. Suffice to say, the affair was to dominate the world's society pages for most of the 1930s.

Twenty years later, the world thrilled to yet another sensational royal romance involving an American lady. This time though, the fairy story was to have a happy ending. The stage for the drama was Monaco, which the French patronizingly call 'the operetta state'. This 370-acre enclave on the sun-drenched French Riviera – ruled by descendants of the 13th-century Genoese family of Grimaldi – was annexed by France during the Revolutionary and Napoleonic eras, and then awarded to Sardinia. However, in 1861 it regained its independence, although – by a Treaty of 1918 – the succession to its throne must be approved by the French government.

The Principality's prosperity derives from tourism and its casino. Originally part of a large house on the sea front, and controlled by the *Société des Bains de Mer*, it used to close its doors at dusk. Then, the only access to it – as to the Principality – was along an appalling coast road. However, in the 1860s Prince Charles III allowed the coast road to be improved and a French coastal rail link to be built through his territory. Seizing the moment, an alert French businessman quickly bought the concession on the failing casino and the surrounding land on which he erected a new casino and a new town – which he named 'Monte Carlo' after the ruling Prince.

The next Prince was Albert, who ruled between 1889–1922. A talented marine biologist, he founded Monaco's noted oceanographic museum and also inaugurated the famous Monte Carlo rally. He was succeeded by his son Prince Louis II, whose daughter Charlotte married Count Pierre de Polignac. Charlotte renounced the throne in favour of her son Rainier who had been born in 1923, so he succeeded on the death of his grandfather in 1949.

Prince Rainier III's marriage plans provoked fascinated press speculation from the moment of his accession, but he was in his early 30s before he met the woman he wished to marry. The lady in question was born in 1929, the daughter of an Irish–American millionaire who had started life as a bricklayer. With her father's talent for success, Grace quickly achieved stardom as a film actress. In 1955 she attended the Cannes Film Festival, held at that famous resort on the French Riviera. At the request of a photographer, Prince Rainier agreed that Miss Kelly might have a photographic session in his palace. That Christmas he visited the United States, where he contrived another meeting. Soon after, at a New Year's Eve party, Rainier proposed and was accepted.

The wedding was set for April, and the press positively bubbled with excitement. One insistent query was whether the Princess would continue to work in films. In an interview in January, the Prince announced she wouldn't. But then the world wondered, was Miss Kelly actually making a film to be released after her marriage? Some said she was; others said she wasn't. In fact *The Swan* – in which she played the part of a princess – did appear when interest in the wedding was at its height. In his own words, the producer 'sat back and waited for the enormous gross' to roll in. However, the public was much more interested in the real life-story of a Hollywood Princess than in any Hollywood version of it.

By the day of the wedding itself, the miniature state was thronged to capacity – there were 1,800 photographers, reporters and TV technicians alone. As the Bride sailed in on the liner *Constitution*, to be met by her royal bridegroom in his yacht *Deo Juvante*, the sky above the crowded harbour blazed with a firework display from the *Christina* – the floating palace of Aristotle Onassis, who had acquired the casino concession the previous year. Nowadays, after a troubled period caused by Onassis' business interests, the Prince presides over a flourishing tourist centre. His heir, Prince Albert, was born in 1958; and in 1978 his eldest child, Princess Caroline – another long-time favourite with the gossip columnists – married a French businessman called Philippe Junot.

Above, *Prince Rainier of Monaco and Grace Kelly, shortly after their engagement.* Centre, *the wedding service of Prince Rainier and Princess Grace.* Right, *their eldest daughter, Princess Caroline.*

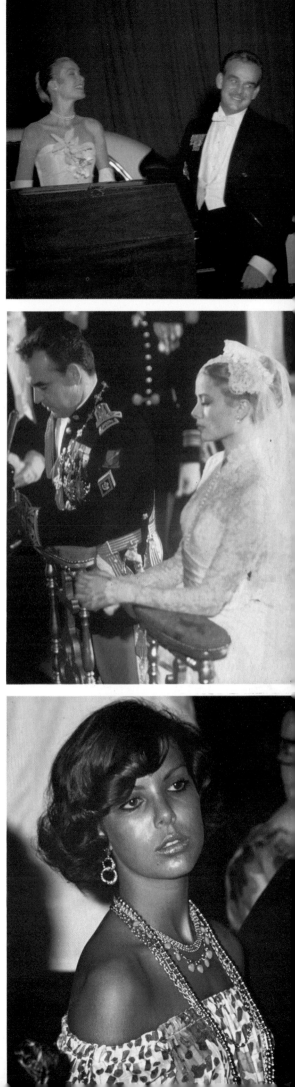

INSTRUMENT OF ABDICATION

I, Edward the Eighth, of Great
Britain, Ireland, and the British Dominions
beyond the Seas, King, Emperor of India, do
hereby declare My irrevocable determination
to renounce the Throne for Myself and for
My descendants, and My desire that effect
should be given to this Instrument of
Abdication immediately.

In token whereof I have hereunto set
My hand this tenth day of December, nineteen
hundred and thirty six, in the presence of
the witnesses whose signatures are subscribed.

SIGNED AT
FORT BELVEDERE
IN THE PRESENCE
OF

All for Love

His face at times wore such a look of beauty as might have lighted the face of a young knight who had caught a glimpse of the Holy Grail.' The words are those of Stanley Baldwin, the British prime minister in 1936; the 'young knight' in question was King Edward VIII in the days following his resolve to marry Mrs Wallace Warfield Simpson.

Edward had been King since the death of his father, George V, on 20 January 1936, and Mrs Simpson received a decree nisi at Ipswich – the birthplace of Henry VIII's minister Cardinal Wolsey – on 27 October. It was her second divorce, and six months after the decree she would be free to wed a third time. At an historic audience on 16 November 1936, Edward informed his chief ministers: 'I intend to marry Mrs Simpson as soon as she is free to marry.' That would be after the date that had already been decided upon for the King's coronation. However, Edward also made it clear at the same meeting, that rather than give up his love he would surrender his Crown.

Edward was then 43, a year older than Wallis Simpson. They had met in 1930, and in September of that year the Prince Edward accompanied Mr and Mrs Simpson on holiday to the South of France. However, by then it was clear to Ernest Simpson that his wife had become the latest royal favourite. He found business reasons to prevent him going with the couple on a cruise in the yacht *Rosaura,* followed by a visit to Switzerland. Needless to say, the world's press was not slow to report this undisguised royal liaison. An American Society diarist, 'Chips' Channon, noted: 'The Prince is obviously infatuated and she, a jolly unprepossessing American, witty, a mimic, an excellent cook, had completely subjugated him . . . She is

madly anxious to storm Society while she is still favourite so that when he leaves her (as he leaves everyone in time) she will be secure.'

Born Wallis Warfield, the future Mrs Simpson came from a prosperous Baltimore family, and she was thrilled to be part of Europe's most exclusive social clique. At first, no doubt, she was content if her friendship with the Prince could guarantee her membership. But it was soon apparent that the Prince's feelings were more than merely social. In August 1936, as King, he invited her to Balmoral. Her train arrived on a day when the King was scheduled to attend a hospital fête at Aberdeen Infirmary. However, his engagement was cancelled on the pretext that 'the King was still in Court mourning for his father'. That day, Edward drove to the station to pick up his guest . . . but many, Scots in particular, noted the fact angrily.

Later that month, the King and Mrs Simpson chartered the yacht *Nahlin* for a cruise in the eastern Mediterranean. The carefree King was photographed dressed only in his 'spick-and-span little shorts, and binoculars', in the sea with Mrs Simpson; out of the sea holding hands with Mrs Simpson; acknowledging shouts of 'Long Live Love' from crowds of tourists and press bystanders. Such loose behaviour from the heir of George V even surprised some of the hard-boiled Americans who eagerly

feasted on that year's rich diet of royal scandal. With characteristic discretion, however, the British press simply made demure references to the King on holiday as 'the younger English tourist to the life' and published few pictures.

In Britain, even as the drama heightened after Mrs Simpson's divorce, knowledge of the King's activities was still largely confined to fashionable gossip among the 'high society' of London. The world's press had long carried headlines like 'Mrs Simpson – Queen of Love' and 'King's Moll Reno'd in Wolsey's Home Town' before the British media relaxed its 'gentlemen's agreement' to not mention 'the King's business' . . . a self-denying ordinance that is probably unique in the history of circulation battles. By the time the crisis hit the British headlines, in fact, the dam was about to burst. Yet, before it did, the King went on a tour of Wales just two days after he had privately declared his intention to renounce the throne. In a moving little speech, he promised a crowd of unemployed miners that he would do what he could to see that they got work.

As Edward made that speech, it must have been apparent – even to him – that he would never be in a position to implement his promise. In fact, a stalemate had been reached because the Church of England – of which the Monarch is the Head – would not allow a divorced person to be re-married in a

church. No priest in Britain would preside over the wedding of Edward and Wallis, and if he delayed his coronation until after their (civil) marriage, then the Archbishop of Canterbury would not crown him King.

Having made his choice to avoid a serious constitutional crisis, Edward took the papers prepared for his formal Act of Abdication to show his mother, Queen Mary, on 9 December 1936. 'I broke down and sobbed like a child,' she recorded in her diary. She truly loved her debonair son. She and King George had stoically accepted both his relaxed attitude to the duties of monarchy which had shaped their own lives and the reports of his numerous love affairs – always with married women. Ruefully, they recognized that such licence was traditionally allowed the heir to the Crown, waiting for the day when he would grow up and see his duty in the same light as them. Wallis, they hoped, would prove to be a passing infatuation like all Edward's other women. They must have had their doubts, however, when their son – now moving into middle age – brought her to be formally presented at Court. On that December morning, Queen Mary, who admitted she had never been able to talk to him like a son, finally realized that she was powerless to change things. Shortly before his death, her husband – with more realism perhaps – had seen that the case was hopeless. Speaking of

'David', as the Prince of Wales was always known in the family, he said: 'He will ruin himself in 12 months.'

During his life, George v – who appeared to his people as the ideal royal father-figure – was an object of awe to his own young family. Once when he was urged to show more affection to his children, he replied: 'My father was frightened of his mother; I was frightened of my father; and I'm damned well going to see that my children are frightened of me.' Not surprisingly, David was in revolt from the first.

World War I had given him a glimpse of ordinary life, but as heir to the crown he had had to remain behind the lines. Nonetheless, other officers had accepted him as 'a proper chap', and after the War – encouraged by press and politicians – he won a 'Prince Charming' reputation. He danced the Charleston like an expert; he had 'taps' fitted to his shoes; and he enhanced his popular reputation with some sympathetic comments on the miseries of the unemployed. Some members of the Establishment feared such stuff was a dangerous betrayal of industrialist and upper-class interests . . . but perhaps they did not really know their man. During the General Strike of 1926, the nearest Britain has come to class war, this democratic Prince cheerfully lent his car (and chauffeur) to ferry copies of *The British Gazette* – a provocative, almost warmongering sheet edited by

Winston Churchill – to strike-bound Wales. Whatever his record at home, though, no one could deny that on his numerous tours through the Empire, Edward proved a golden ambassador of the monarchy and the 'Mother Country'.

In November 1921, the battle-cruiser HMS *Renown,* all flags flying, steamed into Bombay to the thunder of artillery salvos. Aboard was the Prince of Wales, arriving for his State Tour of India. He was welcomed in a specially built gilded pavilion by the Viceroy and the sovereign Princes of India, presenting a kaleidoscope tableau of shimmering silks and jewelled turbans. From there the brilliant procession wound through crowded streets – despite Gandhi's call for a nationwide boycott as a protest against British Imperial rule. Over the blaring band music, the Prince and his party could hear the distant crack of rifle fire as troops drove back protestors aiming to break up the crowds.

Three special trains carried the royal tourists through northern India. The press went first, equipped with its own

Previous pages, *Edward in his robes as Prince of Wales; and the abdication document.* Above left, *being flown over Windsor Castle.* Above centre, *the popular sporting prince.* Above right, *inspecting the Welsh Land Settlement Society's cooperative farm at Boverton.*

travelling post office. The elaborately decorated royal train followed, with accommodation for a 100-strong retinue almost as luxurious as the fabulous royal coach itself. Bringing up the rear was a mixed passenger and freight train carrying an army of servants, flat trucks for the landaus to be used in formal entries to the cities on the route, and closed vans for the Prince's horses and 25 polo ponies lent to him by friendly maharajahs.

The royal progress rolled majestically on through a whirl of polo matches and banquets, tiger shoots and receptions. It visited Nepal and Burma, and then returned to Delhi in mid-February to a banquet at which the Viceroy entertained 150 princes and 13,350 other guests. Yet, just beyond the ancient city, there was a building site of five square miles in extent, where majestic façades rose half-built among mounds of rubble and sand. The Imperial capital of New Delhi was taking shape, but each step towards its completion was also to be marked by another advance towards Indian self-government.

From India the royal party journeyed eastwards through Ceylon, Malaya, Hong Kong and Japan – where Crown Prince Hirohito entertained them with lavish extravagance. At the same time, he managed to prevent Lord Mountbatten, RN, from casting his keen professional eye over a new Japanese battleship. A brilliant naval officer like his father, 'Dickie' Mountbatten was the favourite cousin of the Prince, and had accompanied him throughout the tour. It was fitting that he should have enjoyed this glittering pageant of the British Raj, since 20 years later – as Viceroy – he was to preside over the transition to Indian and Pakistani independence. One of the outstanding scions of a brilliant family, he was a man of overwhelming ambition and somewhat unexpected inventiveness. Dickie was always interested in speed and efficiency and he is credited as the first man to wear a zip on his trousers. His cousin Edward took up the idea, Bond Street followed suit (so to speak) . . . and the rest is history.

Although Americans generally admired Edward for his modern attitudes to all social conventions and not merely those of dress, the Prince of Wales could as casually offend American sensibilities as those of fuddy-duddy England. In September 1924, for example, he and a party of friends attended an international polo match on Long Island, New York. It rained virtually non-stop, which made the Prince irritable. However, the millionaires of the region honoured by the presence of their visitor,

entertained him royally in a series of magnificent yet, as he thought, somewhat starchy parties. By that time he had come to prefer the fun of raucous speakeasies; dancing with short-skirted 'flappers' and drinking bootleg, bathtub gin – not bootleg, vintage champagne. Time and again he and his entourage slipped out early from balls and banquets mounted in his honour at fabulous cost – and possibly even some risk in the face of the USA's 'Probibition' laws – to sample the illicit delights of equally illegal but 'fun' nightclubs. His hosts, and even the press, were almost as 'not amused' as the legendary Queen Victoria on a bad night. Ironically, the British polo team – which followed the royal road of high living and was comprehensively trounced – received a tongue-lashing from the endearing playboy. Back at Buckingham Palace, it is reported, an eavesdropping flunky had once heard the quarter-deck voice of old King George V lambasting, in memorable terms, his wayward heir-apparent: 'You dress like a cad. You act like a cad. You *are* a cad. Get out!' In 1924 there were American hostesses who would have sighed, in principle, a heartfelt 'Hear! Hear!'

For his part, the Prince felt 'chained to the banquetting table'. At the age of 21, he had complained: 'It is sad to say, but I have no real job except that of being Prince of Wales.' And it was sad. Edward was an alert and talented person who was genuinely impatient with the sluggish conventions that rule British society and – in his view – held back British competitiveness in a harsh international environment. His 21st year coincided with the outbreak of World War I, and when he was denied leave to fight on the battlefront, he was quoted as saying: 'What does it matter if I am killed? I have four brothers and it is terrible for me to sit here and see all my friends being killed or wounded.' This was indeed a generous sentiment, but the hard lesson that his enforced inaction during the war never did teach him was that his life ahead would often demand the sacrifice of his personal wishes to public duty.

Nonetheless, after King George's severe illness of 1928, 'David' – as the Prince was always known in the family – began to take a more active part in the ceremonial side of his royal job. Wearing his 'dentist smile', as 'Chips' Channon called it, he assisted his mother at social Court functions, and sometimes received ambassadors presenting their credentials. But the King continued to deny him access to all important State Papers. It seems he knew his son. Later, when the Prince

became King, the government heard with concern that the 'red boxes' of ministerial papers – some containing records of major Cabinet discussions – were regularly taken down in the King's baggage to the fort over the long weekend and there left lying about, casually open to inspection by the numerous guests.

However, from 16 November 1936, when Edward announced his willingness to abdicate, events moved quickly. At first he canvassed the idea of a morganatic marriage: Mrs Simpson would become his wife but not the Queen, and any children they might have would be debarred from the succession. The Prime Minister proposed that before any final decision be taken, the Dominion governments ought to be asked for their advice. The King agreed and, having asked for 'advice', he was constitutionally bound to accept it. Of course the outcome was never in doubt. The prime ministers of Australia, Canada, South Africa and New Zealand

all refused to countenance the marriage.

Some of the King's friends, among them Winston Churchill, urged the formation of a 'King's Party' which could appeal to the country over the heads of the Cabinet. Honourably, and probably wisely too, Edward refused to sanction any such divisive politicking. In any case, as MPs touring their constituencies soon learned, the bulk of popular support was with the government. Then, on the afternoon of Monday, 7 December, Churchill was shouted down as he attempted to argue the King's case. That evening, Mrs Simpson – who had fled the press hubbub which had burst the previous week – announced from Cannes her willingness 'to withdraw from a situation that was both unhappy and untenable'.

But the King's mind was set. On Thursday, 10 December 1936, he signed the Instrument of Abdication. The debate on it in the House of Commons ended with a vote of 403 to 5 in favour of his going. The Bill of Abdication became law next day, signed – like all British laws – by the King himself with the Norman–French words *'Le Roy Le Veult'* – 'The King Wills It'. Edward VIII duly ceased to be King at 1.52 on the afternoon of Friday, 11 December.

That evening, introduced to listeners by Sir John Reith, head of the BBC, as 'His Royal Highness, Prince Edward', he made a touching farewell radio broadcast to the nation. In conclusion he said: 'I have found it impossible to carry the heavy burden of responsibility . . . without the help and support of the woman I love . . . And now we all have a new King . . . God bless you all. God save the King.'

Left, *Edward and Wallis at their wedding in June 1937 at the Château de Condé, near Tours in France.* Below, *King Edward VIII at the microphone for his broadcast to his people in March 1936.*

The Ladies of Orange and Nassau

William III, King of the Netherlands and Grand Duke of Luxembourg, died in 1890. The Dutch Crown then passed to his 10-year-old daughter, Wilhelmina, while Luxembourg – according to the terms of a long-standing family concordat – went to his distant relation, Adolf of Nassau. The accession of Adolf's grand-daughter, Marie-Adelaide, in February 1912, inaugurated 50 years of women's rule in the Grand Duchy.

Luxembourg seemed a fairy-tale country to other, envious Europeans. From the year 1910, the *London Annual Register* of world politics had said quite simply: 'Nothing worth registering happened in this happiest of all countries.' The energetic young Grand Duchess who acceded to the Duchy in 1912 seemed set for a long and happy reign.

However, on 2 August 1914, the idyll shattered as German troops approached the country's neutral frontier. Marie-Adelaide drove to the frontier post and swung her car across the road to bar the way. She radioed to the Kaiser that to trample the Duchy's neutrality would 'sacrifice the honour of Germany'. She then telegraphed her protest to King George of Great Britain. But all her efforts were to no avail.

Like so many royal ladies, Grand Duchess Marie-Adelaide spent the War working as a nurse with the Red Cross. Nonetheless, many of her subjects thought she was also too friendly with the Germans. In June 1917, indeed, she had paid an official visit to the Court of Ludwig III of Bavaria, and the following year she allowed her third sister, Princess Antoinette, to marry the King's son, Prince Rupert. As a result, within days of Germany suing for peace on 11 November 1918, a resolution was passed in the Luxembourg parliament requesting the Grand Duchess to abstain from all political acts until her future should be determined. In 1919 she abdicated, and was succeeded by her sister Charlotte – with the approval of 70% of the voters in a national plebiscite. The following year, Marie-Adelaide entered a Carmelite convent at Modena, Italy.

Twenty-one years later, the family of Grand Duchess Charlotte and her husband, Prince Felix of Bourbon Parma,

were the victims of a cruel, historical repeat performance. During the night of 9 May 1940, news reached the palace at Colmar Berg that German troops were again crossing the frontier. It was decided that the hereditary Duke, Jean, should leave the country with his sisters by one road, while Prince Felix drove the Grand Duchess Charlotte to France. The Duke's party reached safety unmolested, but the other car – which left later – had to crash through a patrol of German soldiers before it too could break free. Despite the ungracious haste of her departure, to have stayed would have presented Charlotte with just the same problems faced by her sister 25 years earlier . . . problems that might have brought her reign to a similarly unhappy end.

On 10 May, a government-in-exile was set up at Luxembourg's legation in Paris. By then, however, France was on the verge of its ignominious capitulation to the *Wehrmacht,* and early in June the government informed the Grand Duchess that it could no longer guarantee her safety. So, driving through France, the royal party crossed into Spain by the bridge at Irun on 18 June. From there they motored on through San Sebastian and south to Lisbon, continental Europe's remaining free, major port. They were not the only royal refugees there. The children of Leopold III of the Belgians and ex-Empress Zita with her son Otto von Habsburg had also arrived in the Portuguese capital that month. In August, Charlotte sailed to London, and from there – with her 88-year-old mother – she went to join Prince Felix in the USA. In May 1941 they travelled to Montreal in Canada, which was also for a time the home of Wilhelmina, the stalwart Queen of the Netherlands.

Wilhelmina, beloved of her people throughout her 50-year reign, wrote in her memoirs of her lifelong endeavour to break out of the 'cage' of monarchy. Although she apparently wanted 'to meet the people as they really were, not dressed for a visit to the palace', Wilhelmina held the noble family of Orange–Nassau from which she was descended in almost mythical reverence.

Orange–Nassau had become the leading princely family in the Netherlands in the mid-16th century, when William 'the Silent' emerged as the hero of a struggle against the colonial power of Spain. William and many of his successors were *Stadholders* – the chief Officers of State in the Dutch provinces. The family's hold on power was interrupted by important republican episodes in Dutch history, but in 1747 William IV – a member of a collateral branch – became an hereditary *Stadholder*. The present royal family descends directly from him.

In fact the Netherlands got its first 'King' in 1806, when Napoleon Bonaparte abolished the 'Batavian Republic' he had set up 10 years before, in order to give his brother Louis a crown. After Napoleon's downfall, the title was legitimated by the Congress of Vienna (1814–15) and conferred on King William I. His state included Belgium and Luxembourg: the former won its independence in the 1830s; the latter was detached from the Dutch Crown with the accession of Wilhelmina.

Wilhelmina's mother Emma, the Queen Regent, trained the child monarch in a strict sense of royal duties, and traits of her dominating personality were not long in revealing themselves. She came of age in 1898, and was inaugurated – according to tradition – in the Nieuwe Kerk, Amsterdam. It was a brilliant occasion, made the more colourful by the exotic robes of the princes of the Netherlands' Indonesian colonies. However, this was a secular ceremony although held in a church. As the Dutch Reformed Church has no bishops, the inauguration of a Dutch monarch omits the ceremony of annointing, which is central to the consecration of a British monarch, for instance. Instead, the central act is the monarch's oath to uphold the constitution and to discharge her royal duties faithfully. The young Queen pledged her word standing before a credence table on which had been placed a crown, sceptre, orb and a copy of the constitution. But these symbols of the royal authority remained in place. The oath was followed, not by a coronation, but by the formal acknowledgement of the new monarch by the President of the Joint Assembly of the States General. With his words – 'We receive you and inaugurate you in the name of the Dutch People' – Wilhelmina became Queen of the Netherlands.

In the first full year of her reign, the new Queen played hostess to the world's diplomatic community at an International Peace Conference held in the Hague. Its principal achievement was to set up the Permanent Court of Arbitration, or 'Hague Tribunal'. Fourteen years later, in 1913, Wilhelmina presided over the opening of the Peace Palace built in the Hague to house the Tribunal. Since 1945, this building – which was financed by Andrew Carnegie, a Scottish–American millionaire-philanthropist – has been the home of the International Court of Justice. However, at the opening ceremony, the Queen's 'cage' was well and truly broken. An American lady, having found the ideal vantage point from which to view the proceedings, was only persuaded with great difficulty that she had in fact occupied the Queen's chair.

Then, in the following year, events in the real world shattered all hope of peace for Europe. By the end of July, only days before the outbreak of war, Wilhelmina telegraphed her husband, Prince Henry, who was on holiday in Oslo. He was back in the capital before the Kaiser, who was cruising in Baltic waters, returned to Berlin. From the start, the Dutch and their Queen were determined to stay neutral. Luckily for them, Holland did not lie directly astride any lines of German advance, but from time to time there were still rumours that the country was about to enter the fray. During these difficult years, the Dutch came to regard their Queen's movements as a particularly reliable barometer of government intentions. On one occasion – in Wilhelmina's view – she put a stop to speculation by the simple expedient of taking a casual morning walk from her palace at Nooreinde to her mother's residence in the Voorhout. If the Queen had time for a stroll, observers reasoned, then there was no crisis.

In fact, Wilhelmina took her royal duties very seriously. At regular meetings with ministers, she insisted on the importance of all Dutch people prominent in either business or diplomacy acting with meticulous impartiality between the combatants. Neither were her regular tours of the frontiers and military installations mere formalities, and even officers conducting night manoeuvres might unexpectedly find their performance being assessed by the watchful eye of their monarch.

For most of the war years the royal family could hear the rumble of distant guns from their pleasant home at Huis ten Bosch. Wilhelmina herself experienced the full force of the canonading when, in 1918, she toured the Zeeland frontier and passed Belgian artillery firing at the faraway enemy. Yet the war's end seemed to threaten her more nearly. As revolution swept through Germany and the Kaiser took refuge in Holland, some thought the House of Orange might also be unseated by Dutch revolutionary social elements. But speculations were laid to rest when the royal family formally made their post-war return to the Hague. Their ceremonial procession was a triumph; the crowd unhitched the horses of the State Coach and dragged it through city streets lined with fervent, cheering patriots.

Strangely, the Queen who had done so much to keep Holland neutral during the war, then seems to have been closely involved in the decision not to hand

Previous pages, *Princess Juliana and Queen Wilhelmina in 1939. A postcard issued just before Juliana's birth.*
Above far left, *the palace, Luxembourg.*
Above left, *Charlotte of Luxembourg and Prince Felix.* Below left, *Wilhelmina and Prince Henry (1903).*
Below, *Wilhelmina's inauguration.*

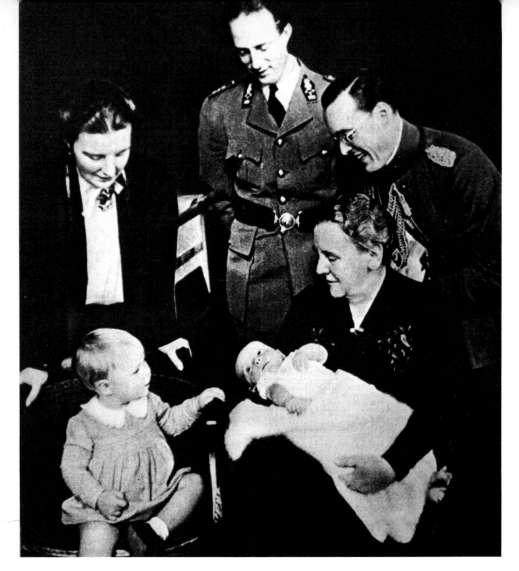

over the refugee Kaiser to the Allies. In her memoirs, Wilhelmina states that she was astonished to hear that William II had crossed the Dutch frontier on 10 November 1918, and herself believed it would have been more honourable of him to stay with his armies in defeat. Once he was on Dutch territory, however, neither she nor her ministers would surrender him for fear that this would impugn Holland's right to grant asylum in the future.

Between the wars it appears that the Queen sensed the growth of a new German threat long before her ministers, but she could do nothing to prevent economies in defence expenditure being imposed by her administrations. Nonetheless, she did order Dutch military attachés abroad to report directly to her on German armaments, and she had senior military advisers brief her regularly in person on the state of Dutch defences.

During the Depression years of the 1930s, the Queen was equally critical of the government's 'adaptation' policies, under which government expenditure was cut and measures were taken to delay the devaluation of the country's currency – with the result that unemployment worsened. In fact, she was so dismayed by the state of the country

and her powerlessness to put things right in her own way that she more than once considered abdicating. She had indeed resolved on this course of action in 1938 – to 'celebrate' the Jubilee of her 40th year of personal rule. In the event, she was only dissuaded from doing so after long arguments with Princess Juliana and Prince Bernhard – the heiress and her consort. That year, the first week in September was devoted to national celebrations. The Queen's apprehensions were shared by few of her citizens, and the Prime Minister complacently observed that European parliamentary democracy only seemed to be secure in those countries that had constitutional monarchies.

The Jubilee year had begun well for the royal family with the birth of a daughter and heiress, Princess Beatrix, to Juliana and Bernhard. The Queen's only regret about this addition to her happy family was that four years before she had lost her own husband Prince Henry of Mecklenburg Schwerin. They had met in 1901, and Wilhelmina soon fell in love with him and his little country set amid the lakes and forest of northern Germany. It was a great disappointment to her that after the revolutions of 1918 – in which the Grand Duchy, like other German states,

was overthrown – she was no longer able to visit her husband's home. Although the royal pair were happily married, the Prince took little share of his wife's duties. In the war, the Red Cross – which was traditionally the province of other countries' Queens – became Prince Henry's concern. His work in its organization showed real abilities but, possibly for political reasons, Wilhelmina was careful not to involve her German husband more closely in government. His death in 1934 was a bitter blow to her and, in a touching tribute, she ordered that his funeral be dressed in white.

Five years later, at the outbreak of World War II, the Netherlands once again hoped to remain neutral. Apart from the flooding of some low-lying border territories, few defensive moves were made for fear of provoking a pre-emptive German attack. But invasion came, nevertheless, on 10 May 1940. Having first gained the consent of the commander-in-chief of the armed forces, Wilhelmina telephoned the King of England to ask him for assistance. Three days later, on the advice of her ministers, she left the Hague for the Hook of Holland where a British warship was waiting. As far as she knew, the plan was for her to be carried to Flushing, where she intended to set up a temporary Seat of Government. However, the British naval captain had orders that he should on no account communicate with the shore, and duly sailed on to Harwich. Wilhelmina, apparently, still hoped to be returned to

her beleaguered country, but instead she found herself ushered onto a train . . . to be greeted at London's Liverpool Street station by King George VI.

She had left so hurriedly that she didn't even have a change of clothes, and had to be fitted out temporarily from the wardrobe of her hostess. At first, she and her family naturally lodged at Buckingham Palace, and her grand-daughter – Princess Irene – was in fact christened in the Palace chapel. But the happy event was clouded by the dire news from home: German terror bombing of Rotterdam, on 15 May, had compelled the Dutch to surrender . . . or stand by and watch the demolition of their entire country. Nevertheless, the majority of the Dutch Home Fleet and airforce had escaped to fight alongside the British, while Holland's East India Navy continued at war in the Pacific – commanded by the exiled royal government in London, and financed in part from Dutch assets in the USA. Throughout the war, the Queen's broadcasts from London – confidently predicting victory – did much to bolster morale in occupied Holland; while in England she became the focus of national loyalty for hundreds of other Dutch exiles, or 'Englandvaarders'.

Wilhelmina did not believe in keeping a low profile, even in exile. On 2 June 1942, when she opened the Dutch Centre in London, she wore her famous marguerite for the first time. This little white flower was quickly adopted by the whole of the exiled Dutch community as an emblem of their national allegiance and solidarity with those suffering oppression in Holland. A few days later, Wilhelmina left for Ottawa to visit Princess Juliana and her family. From there the Queen went to Washington DC, where she addressed Congress on the occasion of the signing of the USA's Lend-Lease agreements with the Netherlands. Like other visiting royalty, she was fêted and received a visit from President Roosevelt.

As the war in Europe drew to a close, Wilhelmina made her triumphal return to the liberated Netherlands on 13 March 1945. Although her courage and example had been widely admired in wartime, and her return was greeted by emotional demonstrations of loyalty, Wilhelmina soon realized that Dutch politics had not changed in her absence. With the re-establishment of constitutional government, her subjects would allow her no more than ceremonial functions. On the other hand, during her exile in London, the Queen's personality had become increasingly forceful in ministerial discussions. So, unable to be content as a mere peacetime figurehead, she abdicated in 1948. Until her death in 1963, she devoted her retirement largely to her religious interests and her memoirs.

At the age of 39, Juliana succeeded her revered mother with the memorable words:'Who am I, that I should be worthy of this?' She had married the German Prince Bernhard of Lippe–Biesterfeld in 1937, and they had four daughters: Beatrix, born in 1938; Irene, born in 1939; Margriet, born in 1943 during the family's wartime evacuation in Canada; and Christina, born in 1947. Prince Bernhard spent much of the war in London. Trained as a pilot, he acted as liaison officer between the Dutch and British forces, and in 1944 was appointed Commander of the Netherlands' army and air force and of the Resistance organizations. After the war, he continued to be a distinguished figure in public life until 1976. Then, as a result of worldwide investigations into the disreputable business methods of the American Lockheed aircraft company, in which he was implicated, Prince Bernhard resigned most of the public offices he held.

Juliana earned her people's affection and respect with her close concern for all aspects of social welfare. Also like her mother, she had become the matriarch of a large and growing family. All her daughters are married, and her heiress, Princess Beatrix, has three sons – Princes William, Constantine and Friso – with Claus von Amsberg, the German diplomat who became her husband in 1966.

Above left, *Wilhelmina holding Princess Irene; Juliana, Leopold III of Belgium and Prince Bernhard (right) look on.* Below left, *the wedding of Princess Beatrix. Guests include ex-king Michael of Romania (extreme left), Constantine II (Greece), Baudouin (Belgium) and Prince Juan Carlos of Spain (third from right at back).* Below, *a gift for the Queen.*

Kings at War

'I have searched my heart and I cannot appoint Quisling, whom I know to enjoy no confidence, either with the people as a whole or with the people's representatives. If, therefore, the government should decide to agree to the German demands, there would not be an alternative for me but to abdicate and renounce the throne of Norway – for me and my House.'

These words, of Haakon VII of Norway, were spoken during a Council meeting in April 1940. That was the only occasion on which Haakon publicly expressed his own opinion before receiving the constitutional advice of his ministers. With them, he kept high the honour of a king, and ensured that the name of Quisling – Norway's fascist leader – should become synonymous with 'traitor'.

In April of 1940, the Nazi war-machine was already grinding through Norway. In the face of overwhelming odds, capitulation seemed the only sensible course of action. King Haakon recognized the dangers of defiance and the dilemma of his government, but it was clear that he could not personally collaborate with the invaders. Although the Council of State finally recommended the Crown to reject Germany's terms, Norway nonetheless succumbed to the inevitable German occupation within a matter of weeks. However, Quisling's regime had no constitutional authority to speak of.

The King and government ministers left Oslo by train on 9 April. They were making for Hamar, 145 km (90 miles) to the north, but 24 km (15 miles) out from Oslo the royal train had to halt because of German air raids. A railway regulation prohibited the movement of all traffic during enemy action, and even with the King aboard the engine driver only consented to move on after he had telephoned the director-general of the railways for authorization. It was a fitting start to a man-hunt for a constitutional monarch.

On 10 April, a broadcast proclamation called on Norwegians to resist the German aggressors. As the figurehead of the Resistance, the King immediately became an important target, and for eight weeks the royal party found itself harried by German airplanes and paratroopers – with orders to take the King

'dead or alive'. When this all-out effort failed, Brauer – the German minister to Norway – was dismissed from the diplomatic service and sent to fight at the front. However, it had been a close thing. At one point the King had to make a dash over the Swedish frontier to avoid German air attack, even though the Swedish government – warily guarding its neutrality – had refused a telephone request for a guarantee of safe passage back to Norway. In the event, a friendly frontier officer connived at his return.

The chase had then continued over appalling mountain roads, with the cars sliding in the melting snow as they jolted on between cliff and precipice. On one occasion the royal party even travelled a short stretch by local train hidden in an empty mail van. Yet the Germans kept frighteningly well informed of their movements. Many Norwegians, while admiring the King's determination to resist, thought he was merely making a quixotic gesture. Often, even those people who helped him were eager for him to move on.

Finally, on 29 April, Haakon boarded the British cruiser HMS *Glasgow* in the port of Molde. On board was a substantial part of the gold reserve of the Bank of Norway. Like some hero of a Norse saga, King Haakon and his treasure sailed northwards through the dangerous seas to Tromso, far beyond the Arctic Circle. But the mayor of the town was not flattered by their arrival, and with the *Luftwaffe* still in pursuit, the royal party moved on. On 17 May, Norway's National Day, they tuned in to the service of remembrance broadcast from the Norwegian Seaman's Church in London. Tears came to the eyes of the stalwart old man as the

preacher concluded with a message of loyalty to the King.

On 9 May, two trawlers steamed into Tromsø carrying the remainder of the Bank of Norway's gold, which had been left behind in the hurried departure from Molde. Although it had been smuggled for a month through occupied Norway, not a single bar of the nation's entire gold reserve had been lost. Nevertheless, the King and government were still in dire jeopardy, especially after the defeat of a British commando operation on the Norwegian coast. So, on 7 June 1940, HMS *Devonshire* steamed out of Tromsø, carrying the royal party to Scotland and safety. They arrived in Greenock on 10 June, and a few days later the BBC Overseas Service proudly announced to the world that Haakon VII of Norway was in London. In fact, until September that year he stayed at Buckingham Palace as a guest of George VI.

Haakon's heroic determination had been in the best tradition of the Norse sagas, but he brought to the Allied cause far more than a fairy-story romance of royal derring-do. Over £36,000,000 of Norwegian gold ensured that this government-in-exile – unlike other royal pensioners from occupied Europe – could definitely pay its own way. During those wartime years, the King gloriously fulfilled the only powerful role still allowed to modern monarchy. For Norwegians throughout the world he symbolized their country's refusal to acknowledge Nazi tyranny. At home the royal cypher – 171 – became a graphic token of defiance scrawled in the snow, on office walls and advertising hoardings. Many Norwegians even braved the North Sea crossing to Scotland in frail open boats, and made their way south to be received by the King in London. And in seaports all over the world, sailors of the Norwegian Merchant Marine acknowledged loyalty only to their King.

By refusing to collaborate with Nazism, Haakon brought not only gold but also 1,000 ships to aid the Allied cause. This vast fleet was administered from the Norwegian Shipping and Trade Mission in London, and the director kept his friend, the King, closely informed of its work. As one British government minister later reflected: 'I often wonder how things would have gone if Norway had not resisted German occupation – if Norway had done as stronger nations did and said, "What's the use?" Two-fifths of the petrol coming to Britain is carried in Norwegian tankers, which are now playing the same role in the Battle of the Atlantic as the spitfires did in the Battle of Britain.'

However, soon after his arrival in Britain, Haakon received a letter from King Gustav of Sweden urging him to abdicate. Under German pressure, the Norwegian Storting (parliament) next formally requested his abdication. In reply, on 8 July, Haakon broadcasted a message of defiance and encouragement which was secretly printed and distributed throughout his country. In England, meanwhile, the tall and grizzled figure of this venerable old man who had been a monarch since 1905 soon became well known. For much of the war he lived at Foliejon Park near Windsor, travelling regularly to London to do his own shopping and conduct the business of government with his ministers at the Norwegian embassy. After Councils of State he lunched at the Norwegian Club and mingled with men and women from his own country, or at the Senior United Services Club where he chatted with Norwegian officers. He travelled throughout Britain, visiting Norwegian organizations or inspecting the Norwegian Army's training camp at Dumfries in Scotland.

Soon after he arrived in Britain, a BBC receptionist, putting through a call for the King in Broadcasting House, London, turned to him with the question: 'Where was it you said you were King of?' In contrast, by the end of the war, Haakon was almost as well known to Londoners as he was to his own people. His return to Norway on 7 June 1945 – five years to the day after his flight into exile – was a triumph for both him and his country. When he died in September 1957, at the age of 85, he was mourned by many British friends as well as by the whole of Norway.

King Olav V, 76 years old, who acceded in 1957, went to Balliol College, Oxford. He made an international reputation in sport, being an expert skier and winning a gold medal in the 6-metre (20-foot) yachting event in the 1928 Olympic Games. In 1929 he married Princess Martha of Sweden who died tragically 25 years later. Crown Prince Harald (born 1937) now shares the royal duties; his heir by his wife Princess Sonia is the young Prince Haakon.

Previous pages, *King Haakon VII of Norway and Queen Maud*. Left, *King Haakon VII of Norway in exile 'somewhere in England' during World War II*. Above left, *Haakon VII and Queen Maud, photographed with Crown Prince Olav*. Above, *the christening of Princess Martha Louise*.

A year after the veteran Haakon was received at Buckingham Palace, King George played host to 18-year-old Peter II of Yugoslavia. For seven years the young King had been an increasingly alert observer of the tangled politics of his troubled state. Then, on 26 March 1941, the government of Regency under his uncle Paul signed a pact with Germany. Ministers explained to the young King that Yugoslavia could not hope to withstand the Nazi war-machine, and that this agreement would assure the integrity of the country until he came of age in September and could determine his own policy. But the very next day a military *coup* toppled the Regent and proclaimed Peter the country's acting ruler. However, he had barely a week to enjoy his reign unmolested. Then, on 6 April, the *Luftwaffe* began strafing Belgrade.

Of course the Yugoslav air force was hopelessly outnumbered, but it was also equipped in part with German-built machines. As a result, the young monarch had to stand by helplessly as his own pilots repeatedly fired on one another in mistake for the enemy. To add to his problems the palace air-raid alarm was soon out of action and Peter had to post a trumpeter on the roof with orders to blow a call the moment he saw enemy aircraft approaching. A week later, as German armies rolled towards

Belgrade from the north and east and from across the Bulgarian frontier, the royal government bowed to the inevitable and fled the capital.

The intention was to set up a rival government at a secret mountain HQ but – panicked by the inexorable German advance – on April 13, Peter climbed aboard an aircraft waiting on an improvised runway at Niksic in the Montenegrin mountains. The next day he was being received in Athens by his uncle, King George II of Greece. Although the Greek Court was in turmoil, and the country itself was on the verge of collapse under the onslaught of Germany's Balkan offensive, a villa was nonetheless made available to Peter at Kephisia, near the capital. He stayed there for a few days before being flown in an RAF Sunderland flying-boat to Alexandria in Egypt. From there he and his little entourage were flown to Jerusalem, and it was suggested at first that he set up his government-in-exile in British-mandated Palestine. So, for six weeks, the King at Jerusalem and his 'Court' in the nearby monastery of Tantura went through the motions. But no one believed in the farce. After another 15 days spent in Cairo, Peter was flown to England where – on 28 June – the BBC broadcast his call for resistance to the people of Yugoslavia.

Royalist Serbian armed resistance

was led by the Cetniks under General Mihailovič, whom Peter appointed his minister of war in January 1942. Yet even a common, barbarous enemy could not close the rifts between the rival components of the Yugoslav nation. Although Peter frequently broadcast messages of unity and common purpose to his beleaguered people, the politicians in his London 'cabinet' continued the struggles of Serb and Croat. Meanwhile, in the mountains of Yugoslavia, the Cetniks found themselves competing for the loyalty of the peasants with communist partisans led by Tito. No doubt, the King's exile from the patriotic conflict greatly weakened his cause, while the communists also accused Mihailovič and his people of collaborating with the Germans and using terrorism against the peasants.

At first, though, the King at least enjoyed the free support of the Western Allies. In his memoirs, *A King's Heritage,* he recalls happy visits to the family of his 'Uncle Bertie' (King George VI), several meetings with Winston Churchill, and an encouraging visit to President Roosevelt in Washington. But appearances were deceptive, and Peter became increasingly embittered as he realized that his 'friends' were gradually switching their support to the communist cause and the interests of Stalin, their Russian ally.

Despite his involvement in high politics, Peter was still only of student age. It was decided he should continue his education at Clare College, Cambridge. There, the undergraduate King was allowed the then-exceptional privilege of running a car. But he also used more conventional student transport, and bought himself a truly 'kingly' bicycle. Within days it was stolen, but when a friend explained the communistic principles that governed the use of student cycles, the King promptly stole himself another – less grand – model.

However, studies of economic and international law hardly gripped the royal interest. Instead, Peter persuaded the British government to organize commando training for Yugoslav officers who had escaped from German prison camps, and himself spent all the time he could flying. In June 1944, without seeking official permission, he flew a photo-reconnaissance mission deep into northern France from an American air base in Southern England. On the return journey, 'at the suggestion of the co-pilot', they took a 'flip' over German-occupied Paris. When they got back to base a flustered base commander begged the King, 'for Pete's sake', not to enter the trip in his flying log. Pete – the King – agreed.

For the young King, this story-book exploit came as a welcome break from his deepening dispute with Churchill over the future of Yugoslavia. Using communist claims of Cetnik atrocities to buttress his decision, Churchill eventually told Peter that if he continued to oppose Tito's aims he would henceforth be regarded as opposing the Allies' war-effort. However, Peter was too young to accept such harsh realities of power politics, and he naively continued to seek constitutional guarantees for his own position in post-war Yugoslavia. On the other hand, Churchill was only concerned that he would appoint Regents who – while supposedly acting on his behalf – would give Tito's assumption of power the seal of royal approval. At last Churchill lost his patience with the stubborn young monarch. In a speech in the House of Commons in January 1945, he asserted: 'We have no special interest in the political regime in Yugoslavia. Few people in Britain, I imagine, are going to be more cheerful or more downcast because of the future constitution of Yugoslavia.' This was hardly the emotional oratory of constitutional liberties with which the same Prime Minister regularly inspired his own people!

In fact, from the moment Britain and the USA decided to support Tito, King Peter's cause had been hopeless. In his heart of hearts he must have known this, yet he was careful to observe due protocol at the birth of his son and heir in July 1945. Accordingly, a group of commissioners from the London government-in-exile were summoned to attend the birth. They stood, embarrassed, in a room adjoining the Queen's bedroom, and 30 minutes after the birth they signed a formal statement to certify that Queen Alexandra had borne a son. The paper-work was in order and the House of Karageorge had an heir; but few outside that room believed any longer in the Kingdom of Yugoslavia of which this infant happened to be the Crown Prince.

King Peter II of Yugoslavia. Above far left, in Yugoslav uniform while a student at Clare College, Cambridge, with Sir Henry Thirkill, Master of the College, March 1942. Above left, inspecting a guard of honour at Hampstead, August 1942, before a function to raise funds for the Yugoslav relief fund. Left, with his bride, Princess Alexandra of Greece, March 1944.

In retrospect, the Yugoslavian monarch's slide into oblivion began when German tanks first rumbled over its frontiers four years earlier. Hitler's *blitzkrieg* offensive owed much to his military bases in Bulgaria, which had been handed over by Tsar Boris III. 'My generals are pro-German,' Boris observed, 'my diplomats are pro-British, my Queen is pro-Italian and my people are pro-Russian.' Nevertheless, both sentiment and policy demanded an *entente* with Germany. Boris had family ties with fascist Italy through his father-in-law, Victor Emmanuel III; Russia, honoured by Bulgarians as their historic liberator from the Turks, was in alliance with Germany; Britain was soon to prove unable to assist even Greece; and – the most compelling argument of all – an alliance with Germany would mean the recovery of Macedonia . . . which every Bulgarian government for 60 years had dreamed of in vain.

In December 1941 Hitler finally tightened the screws, and Boris had to declare war on Britain and the USA – though he refused to do so against Russia. Feeling 'like a caterpillar beneath the raised foot of an elephant', he continued to wriggle through the deadly undergrowth of wartime diplomacy until – in August 1943 – Hitler peremptorily demanded his presence at German HQ. The details of the meeting in Berlin are still unclear but, almost certainly, Hitler demanded more wholehearted Bulgarian commitment to the war.

Back in Sofia on 17 August, Boris claimed that despite terrible pressure he had nevertheless been able to safeguard Bulgaria's interests. Four days later he complained of dizziness and, on 28 August, he died. The official cause of death was given as a heart attack, but many people believed that German agents had murdered him.

In the same year, 1943, Italy was facing defeat as the reluctant ally of Germany. King Victor Emmanuel III had come to the throne of Italy in 1900 after the assassination of his father, Umberto I. He had led his troops bravely during World War I, but his failure to authorize martial law in 1922 assured the triumph of the fascists 'March to Rome' and Mussolini's coming to power. For the next 20 years Victor Emmanuel played the role of constitutional monarch, receiving the dictator in audience each Monday and Thursday.

There had been whispers of a royalist anti-fascist *coup* as early as 1942. Undoubtedly, though, the King was the key to any successful move. As the 'moderate' fascist Count Dino Grandi reflected: 'Only the King at the right moment can restore things to their place.' In February 1943, 84-year-old General Zuppelli eagerly urged his monarch to chase Mussolini out 'on the

spot'. But Victor Emmanuel knew he would not get a second chance if he miscalculated. In the words of another fascist malcontent: 'So long as the situation is handled under the aegis of the dynasty, its solution will have a legal character and the troops will obey their orders.' Of course this was vital to forestall anarchy and the possibility of a fascist anti-coup. Timing was all.

Then, on 19 July, Hitler and Mussolini met urgently in a secluded villa near Treviso in northern Italy. The recent Allied invasion of Sicily had put Mussolini under heavy pressure from his military advisers to negotiate a separate peace, but Hitler refused to even contemplate this happening. On his return to Rome, Mussolini called a special meeting of the fascist Grand Council for the evening of Sunday, 24 July. At this periodic assemblage, his henchmen generally met to be informed of their leader's thoughts. In Mussolini's own words, there was 'never, I repeat never, any question of voting'.

Nevertheless, in the early hours of Monday, 25 July, Count Grandi proposed a motion critical of 'the regime' which was approved by a majority. Mussolini appeared unconcerned, and

the next day prepared for his usual audience with the King at 5.00 pm. But the *coup* was now gathering momentum. At three o'clock the King authorized the arrest of the Duce after the audience. Because he didn't know what reaction to expect from the Duce, he asked his military household adviser 'to stand by the door of the drawing-room where we shall talk', and told him 'to intervene if need arises'.

In the event, the need did not arise. Mussolini arrived punctually and began his report. Victor Emmanuel interrupted him, and in a few disjointed sentences – with characteristic lapses into Piedmontese dialect – he demanded the dictator's resignation. The Duce offered no resistance as he was driven away under escort.

Above left, *Prince Regent Paul of Yugoslavia and Boris III of Bulgaria.* Above centre, *Boris and Queen Giovanna of Bulgaria walking down Piccadilly, London, September 1938.* Below left, *Queen Elena of Italy.* Below, *with King Victor Emmanuel III being welcomed at Dover, England in 1924.*

However, even democratic countries in the 20th century have seen their kings in the role of war leaders. For instance, on Monday, 3 August 1914, King Albert of the Belgians made his famous ride on horseback through the flag-crowded streets of Brussels to announce to Parliament the country's rejection of a German demand for free passage of its troops across neutral Belgium to the French frontier. 'One duty alone is imposed upon us,' said the King in a moving and historic speech, '... the maintenance of a stubborn resistance.' He then sent an appeal for support to his royal cousin, George v of Great Britain, but the British government had by then already decided on war with Germany.

Modern Belgium was inaugurated in 1839 by the Treaty of London, under the terms of which Britain guaranteed Belgian independence. Twenty-four years before, the Congress of Vienna had incorporated the territory with Luxembourg in the newly-formed Kingdom of Holland. However, most Belgians bitterly resented this settlement, and the country finally won its independence by revolution in 1830.

Prince Leopold of the German House of Saxe–Coburg, a beloved uncle of Queen Victoria, was elected King. On Britain's insistence, the new state was given international guarantees of neutrality. So, when the Kaiser's troops violated that neutrality in 1914, both honour and self-interest impelled Britain to declare war against Germany.

Leopold I's grandson, King Albert I, was an engagingly democratic monarch. During a visit as Crown Prince, to the USA, he donned overalls and rode the footplate on the train journey from New York to St Louis. However, his forceful father, King Leopold II, had little sympathy with such egalitarian escapades. On one occasion – so the story goes – when the Prince knocked some papers from his father's desk onto the floor, the King sourly stopped the courtier who had bent to pick them up with the words: 'A future constitutional monarch must learn to stoop.'

Nonetheless, Albert I had a truly royal presence, and he was to inspire his soldiers and people with his example during the Great War. At first, Kaiser William of Germany had hoped to persuade him and his German-born wife, Princess Elizabeth of Bavaria, to bring Belgium into the German camp. In reply, the King joined his army. Then, with German troops triumphant in 'neutral' Liége, William urged him to name his terms for a new settlement, and 'pledged his honour' to carry them out. Albert responded scornfully: 'Were I tempted for one moment to consider your proposals, your assurance would make me hesitate.'

Albert spent most of the war at the front. In army greatcoat or in battle dress, he visited the trenches to the delight of astonished troopers. Once, as he and King George v were touring the cratered battlefield, a wounded soldier stumbled on his crutches and the monarchs bent down to help him to his feet. Ruminating on the incident later, the soldier mused: 'What chance has Jerry got? No sooner does one of his bullets knock a chap down than two kings pick him up again.'

During the four years of war, the royal family became a talisman for the whole country. Royal portraits sold by the thousand, and when their sale was banned, mothers began to sew medallions of the Queen's portrait into their children's clothing. Queen Elizabeth worked devotedly and professionally as a Red Cross nurse. On one occasion, when the Prince of Wales was watching her deft fingers dress a severe shrapnel wound, he mistook the bending figure for that of a professional nurse. In July 1918, the last summer of the war, the

King and Queen flew to England to attend the Silver Wedding celebrations of King George and Queen Mary. Then, on 21 July, they celebrated Belgium's independence day at a service in Westminster Abbey. They had been immensely popular in England throughout the war, as the embodiment of 'plucky little Belgium' or – in the lofty words of *The Times*: 'The soul of loyalty to a word pledged, high minds not cast down by long misfortune.'

After the war, Albert and Elizabeth received a tumultuous welcome on a State Visit to America. During the years of peace that followed, Albert keenly supported government measures of social reform. The death of Albert in a

Left, *Leopold II of the Belgians*. Right, *King Albert and Queen Elizabeth of the Belgians landing at Farnborough on their 1920 visit to England*. Below, *King Albert and Queen Elizabeth with their children*. Below right, *the Queen of the Belgians visits the front in World War I.*

rock-climbing disaster at the age of 59 was an occasion of deep national mourning. The following year, another tragedy hit the royal family when the new King, Leopold III, lost his wife, Princess Astrid of Sweden, in an automobile accident. It was a sad omen to an unhappy reign.

As Nazi Germany grew in strength, little Belgium, hoping to avert the tragedy of 1914–18, declared her neutrality and in 1937, Germany guaranteed it. King Leopold and Wilhelmina of the Netherlands vainly sought to mediate at the outbreak of World War II. When Germany once again invaded Belgium in May 1940, King Leopold headed the national resistance. In the conditions of *blitzkrieg* it was pointless and, overriding his Cabinet, the King surrendered unconditionally. He thus saved his country from the holocaust.

His reward was to be accused of treason by many of his countrymen and to be placed under house arrest by the Germans at the castle of Laeken. In 1944 he was taken to Germany where he was liberated the following year by Allied troops. Parliament refused Leopold permission to return home and while he went into exile in Switzerland, his brother, Prince Charles, assumed the Regency.

A referendum in 1950 showed a small majority in favour of Leopold's restoration but his arrival in Belgium sparked off such violent demonstrations that he transferred the royal powers to his son Baudouin and in July 1951 formally abdicated.

King Baudouin and his Spanish wife, Queen Fabiola, whom he married in 1960, are models of modern royalty. The Queen, popular and widely travelled, is a fluent linguist. The King, who is a fine photographer, begins his working day at nine and freely gives audience to his subjects. Unhappily they have no children and the succession will probably pass to Prince Philippe, the eldest son of the King's brother, Prince Albert of Liège and his wife Donna Paola of Italy.

Above far left, *Leopold III of the Belgians and his wife Astrid of Sweden in 1927.* Below far left, *Leopold and Astrid attending the first national fête after their accession in 1934.* Above centre, *demonstrations in Brussels on 31 July 1950 against the return of Leopold III.* Above right, *Leopold at the royal palace, Brussels, with Prince Baudouin and Prince Albert, in 1950, the year before his abdication.* Below centre, *King Baudouin takes the oath.* Left, *his marriage to Queen Fabiola in 1960.*

Back in 1914, when Britain declared war against Germany on 4 August, Queen Alexandra had taken her son – King George V of England – by his coat lapels and shaken him in an anger of frustration, saying: 'I told you so, I told you Willie was the very Devil.' In fact she had been nursing a personal vendetta against Germany ever since, 50 years before, Prussian armies deprived her native Denmark of the Duchies of Schleswig and Holstein – a third of the national territory. At the time, her English family were naturally outraged on her behalf, but their ties with the German royal family and Britain's long-standing desire for friendship with Germany has caused many painful scenes at home and frequent embarrassment abroad. Poor Alexandra, was – at last – to see her prophecies justified. Her brother, Frederick VIII, had fought when a Prince in that earlier war against the Prussians. Now it was for her nephew, King Christian X, to preside over a nation determined to maintain its neutrality.

Christian was 42 when he came to the Throne of Denmark in 1912. Two years later, in December 1914, he met with his colleagues Haakon VII of Norway and Gustavus VI of Sweden at Malmö for the first of a series of meetings they held throughout World War I. In the end, all three countries managed to successfully defend their neutrality, and Denmark even gained out of the conflict when northern Schleswig voted by referendum to return to Denmark in 1920. Fortunately, Queen Alexandra had lived to see this compensation for the wrongs of 1864. But another threat to Denmark's royal domain was already looming large. In 1918, the former Crown Dependency of Iceland was declared to be a sovereign state in union with Denmark . . . but with the right to withdraw. Many Danes were to resent the fact that Iceland chose to exercise that right in 1944, at a time when the Mother Country was in the grip of Nazi domination. Yet from the Icelanders' point of view, the German invasion of Denmark presented them with an ideal opportunity to usurp this residual royal Danish power and take control of their own foreign affairs at the same time.

When Germany began its brief victory parade through continental Europe in 1939, there was little hope that Denmark would again be able to preserve its neutrality as it had in 1914-18. Air power, the mobile nature of the land war, and effective operation of the German U-boat fleet, all required control of the Danish peninsula which juts out strategically from the north German coast. The inevitable ultimatum from Germany came in April 1940, and the Danish government saw no option but to concede.

From then on, the King's government continued in his name, but under German control. Nevertheless, German hopes of Danish cooperation were soon dashed as underground resistance groups formed to sabotage munitions works, railways and port installations. Moreover, with tacit government approval, resistance 'pipelines' were used to smuggle the majority of Denmark's Jewish population to safety in Sweden.

Throughout the German occupation, King Christian was the emblem of his country's will to resist. Almost daily he was to be seen proudly riding his white horse through the streets of the capital. He withstood all Nazi demands for anti-Jewish legislation but could not, as Head of State, refuse to appeal against the acts of sabotage – which the Germans inevitably viewed as terrorism. However, as he would not agree to hand over Danes to the courts in Germany, the exasperated Germans finally declared martial law in August 1943. Although the King was placed under house-arrest in his palace, this apparently decisive move soon bogged down in canny Danish constitutionalism. Initially, the whole government resigned in protest. But then Christian IX refused either to accept the resignation or to appoint a new cabinet. As a change of government could only be made with the approval of parliament – which had of course been suspended at the request of the occupying forces – the result was that Denmark was left without any legislative body of its own. For three years the Germans had attempted to cloak their regime in legalism, but the charade was now finally over.

When he died in 1947, the beloved and quietly heroic King Christian had been brought – in the ordeal of war – closer to his people than any previous Danish monarch. He was succeeded by his 48-year-old son, Frederick IX, who was to stamp the monarchy with its modern

democratic image. Each year on his birthday (11 March), the citizens of Copenhagen gathered in the square of the Amalienborg Palace to give their King the day's greetings. Frederick also held regular and frequent audiences open to any of his subjects with a reasonable petition or matter to discuss. Moreover, with their frequent foreign tours and royal visits, he and his Queen – the Swedish-born Ingrid – soon became as popular abroad as at home. Then, in 1953 – with the concurrence of his brother who was at the time the Heir Apparent – Frederick approved a change in the Danish constitution that re-admitted women to the succession. Crown Princess Margarethe became a member of the Council of State in 1958.

Margarethe came to the throne in January 1972, five years after her marriage to Comte Henri de Laborde de Monpezat. Before the end of the year, her people had voted by referendum to enter the European Economic Community – of which, at the moment, more than half the member states are monarchies. How long the exclusive sovereignty they symbolize can survive the federalist dreams of Europe's politicians is, however, by no means clear. Nonetheless, in May 1975 Margarethe II – namesake of the great 14th-century Danish Queen who briefly united all the Scandinavian crowns – became the first European monarch to make a State Visit to the Soviet Union. It was a fitting gesture for the descendant of a family which had provided Russia itself with two Empresses.

Above far left, *King Christian X of Denmark. A familiar sight in the streets of wartime Copenhagen, the mounted King became a silent symbol of Danish patriotism. Second left, King Frederick IX of Denmark. Third left, Frederick IX and Queen Ingrid of Denmark and their daughters Princess (later Queen) Margarethe, Princess Benedikte and* *Princess Anne Marie, who married King Constantine II of the Hellenes, on board the royal yacht, Danneborg. Top right, Margarethe acknowledges the plaudits of the crowd after her proclamation as queen in January 1972. Above, Frederick and Ingrid and their daughters, left to right, Margarethe, Benedikte and Anne Marie.*

Greek Dynasty

❧❧❧❧❧❧❧❧❧❧❧❧❧❧❧❧❧❧❧❧❧❧❧❧❧❧❧❧❧❧❧❧❧

In December 1922, Prince Philip of Greece, future officer of the Royal Navy and Duke of Edinburgh, made his first voyage in a British man-of-war. At the time, he was 18 months old – and travelling in an orange-box. He was, in short, a refugee. His plight was common enough for members of the Greek royal house, and indeed a wit had once remarked that 'he who would be King of Greece should keep his bags packed'.

❧❧❧❧❧❧❧❧❧❧❧❧❧❧❧❧❧❧❧❧❧❧❧❧❧❧❧❧❧❧❧❧❧

The chain of events which brought the little Prince Philip of Greece and his family safely to England in 1922 from their summer home of *Mon Repos* on the island of Corfu, is noteworthy even for that much-travelled dynasty.

The story began on 22 August, when Turks under the generalship of Mustafa Kemal comprehensively routed a Greek army outside the city of Izmir (formerly Smyrna) on the west coast of Turkey. This defeat marked the end of a disastrous and hopelessly mismanaged campaign against Greece's 'old enemy', which had been launched to popular acclaim by Philip's uncle, King Constantine I. The King duly went into exile for the second time; while back at home the army staged a revolution under the leadership of one General Pangolas. A lot of trials followed, as a result of which five politicians and one general lost their lives. Then, on December 2, Philip's father Prince Andrew – who had been a lieutenant-general in the war – stood before a court in the Chamber of Deputies with little hope of a better fate. The trial ended at midnight . . . with a sentence of death.

Meanwhile a British agent, Captain Talbot, had been despatched to plead for mercy on behalf of Prince Andrew with General Pangalos. In view of the court's judgement it seemed he had failed. However, the following morning a British warship anchored in Phaleron Bay . . . and the sentence was commuted. The Prince and his family were stripped of their Greek nationality and condemned to exile for life. The business thus concluded, Pangalos himself drove them down to the dockside where they embarked on the Royal Navy's light cruiser HMS *Calypso*.

Of course the warship had not been in Greek waters merely by chance. On the arrest of her husband back in October,

Princess Alice had rushed to Athens where her 33-year-old nephew, George II, had recently taken over as King from his exiled father, Constantine. However, George's grip on the throne was precarious, and he could do nothing to help free Prince Andrew. But Alice – who was known as a somewhat eccentric lady – was determined . . . and she was also a great grand-daughter of Queen Victoria. She wrote at once to her cousin, King George V of Great Britain. Hence the presence of Captain Talbot at the trial. Hence also the arrival of HMS *Calypso*.

King George had – in an almost certainly unconstitutional exercise of his royal authority – simply put a call through to the Admiralty and ordered a ship be sent at all speed to rescue his relations. The result was an escapade of gunboat diplomacy worthy of Hollywood. Fortunately, though, the Royal Navy arrived in the nick of time. With Andrew and Alice safely aboard, HMS *Calypso* steamed to Corfu to pick up their family of now stateless persons, including the baby Prince. Accommodation is tight in a warship; hence the orange-box.

The story of Greek monarchy began in 1832. In that year, after a long struggle to gain its independence from the Turkish Empire, Greece eventually won the recognition of the Great Powers of Europe. The Powers chose – and the Greeks provisionally accepted – Otto, the 17-year-old second son of King Ludwig I of Bavaria, to inaugurate the new Kingdom with the title 'King of the Helenes.' However, Otto soon ran into trouble. Not only was the Regency Council run by Bavarians, but the King also proved to be unpleasantly authoritarian. A military coup forced him to promulgate a constitution in the 1840s, and he was finally deposed in 1862.

Learning from their mistake, the Greeks elected their next King for themselves. He was another 17-year-old foreigner, Prince William of Denmark, of the royal Danish House of Schleswig–Holstein–Sonderburg–Glucksburg. Months later, the young man's father acceded to the throne of Denmark as Christian IX. Christian is a patriarchal figure in the chronicle of modern European monarchy. Through his daughter, Dagmar, he was a grandfather of Tsar Nicholas II; through another daughter, Alexandra, who married King Edward VII of Great Britain, he was an ancestor of the House of Windsor, and through his grandson, Haakon VII, his line also includes the royal family of Norway.

As a gesture to his new subjects, the young Danish Prince adopted the name of George, who is one of the principal Saints of the Greek Orthodox Church. Guided by his ministers, he introduced a new constitution in the year of his accession. Soon after this he married the Russian Grand Duchess Olga, and the royal couple – with their seven children – went on to live the happy, full lives of Europe's international 'royal set'. In fact the marriage of their second son, Prince Andrew, to Princess Alice of Battenberg – at Darmstadt in October 1903 – was a regular royal gathering of the clans.

On their wedding day, the streets leading from the railway station of the old German town rattled to the hooves and harnesses of state escorts, leading carriage after resplendent carriage bearing royalty of all degrees and ranks. They ranged from minor German princes to 35-year-old Tsar Nicholas II and his radiant Empress, Alexandra Feodorovna. Prince Henry of Prussia, the Kaiser's brother, was also there, along with Queen Alexandra of England, the bridegroom's aunt. Andrew's parents, King George and Queen Olga of Greece, were only in their early 50s – yet they were among the oldest in this gathering.

Prince Louis of Battenburg, the 49-year-old father of the bride, was also one of the older royals who gathered for that glittering day in Darmstadt. He had made his life in England, where he was one of the most brilliant and devoted officers in the Royal Navy, and on

Previous pages, *Constantine I of the Hellenes; the Greek royal guard.*
Above left, *the 8-year-old Philip of Greece, second from left, at the Mac-Jannet American School, St Cloud, near Paris.* Right, *Frederick VIII of Denmark and his brother William, Greek king as George I.*

his way to becoming First Sea Lord. His wife was Princess Victoria, a grand-daughter of the late Queen Victoria. When she gave birth to Alice in the afternoon of 15 February 1885, the old Queen had herself been at the bedside in Windsor Castle. Now Prince Louis had, naturally enough, chosen the Battenberg family town for the wedding of his daughter. There, he installed his own family at his Palace of Heiligenberg, since those of his brother-in-law – the Grand Duke Ernest of Hesse-Darmstadt – were full because most of the guests had brought their children.

The Tsar even brought the Imperial Russian choir with him ... and they were needed. The marriage was celeb-rated three times: the German civil ceremony was followed by a Protestant wedding service, and that by the sonor-ous, chanting rites of the Greek Orthodox Church. The Darmstadt

Opera was a highlight of the days of festival.

No doubt, however, the children pre-ferred the bridal dinner in the banquet-ting hall of the Grand Duke's old palace. This too had music, though of the cheerful, bandstand variety. But when the exhausted, red-liveried serv-ants had cleared away the last of the 10 courses, the toasting began. With half the royal families of Europe represent-ed, a lot of healths had to be drunk. While the grown-ups emptied their cups with increasing liberality, the children scampered about the great hall. At one point, 14-year-old Prince George of Greece – later King George II – crowned a flustered Grand Duchess with a gold-braided cocked hat, while Queen Alexandra of England stood by helpless with laughter.

Meanwhile, the bride and groom seemed to take a ridiculously long time changing into their travelling clothes.

Then at last they appeared, dashing down the grand staircase through a barrage of rice and old slippers. Outside the great doors the waiting landau was sparkling under the blaze of electric lighting. The coachman whipped up his horses and they clattered away from the hoard of pursuing royal relatives. Inside their coach, the newly-weds were no doubt collecting their dignity for the serried ranks of loyal citizens lined up in the road ahead. Then, suddenly, there was an upheaval on the highway. A mob of coronetted and gold-braided rioters burst through the crowds of orderly townsfolk – little princesses and princelings squeezed between their legs. The charge was headed by the Tsar. Nicholas had spotted a side gate across the castle courtyard, and had led the hue-and-cry through this short-cut with the shout: 'We can catch them outside again.' Now, breathless and weak from laughing, he lobbed a last

slipper into the sedately moving carriage. Princess Alice leaned out of the landau and clouted the Tsar with the heel. 'You,' she said, 'are a silly old donkey.'

Sadly, such happy scenes were soon to fade into the sepia-toned mists of history. In 1913, after years of fighting the Turks, the Greeks forced them to cede the island of Crete. Then, while driving in a victory parade through the streets of Salonika on 18 March, King George I – Prince Andrew's father – was shot by a deranged assassin. His eldest son Constantine succeeded to the throne with his wife, Sofia of Prussia – sister of the German Kaiser. The next year, World War I broke out. The Greek Prime Minister, Venizelos, strongly favoured the Allied cause; not unnaturally, Constantine was pro-German. So the King forced Venizelos to resign.

However, the Allies needed Greece in order to pursue their war in the Balkans. As a result, Constantine I and his family woke up one morning in June 1917 to find their palace being bombarded by British warships. In response to this ruthless hint, the King sought refuge in Switzerland – leaving his second son, Alexander, to be installed in his place. His eldest son, George – was passed over because he shared his father's sympathies for Queen Sophia's family. With Constantine out of the

Left, *the funeral of George I, 1913. Assassinated during a parade in Athens to celebrate Greek victory over the Turks, the King's body was borne on a captured Turkish gun carriage. Above, Balkan heirs. Left to right: Alexander of Serbia, Boris of Bulgaria, Constantine of Greece, Ferdinand of Romania and Danilo of Montenegro. Right, Prince Alexander of Greece, later king as Alexander I.*

way, Venizelos returned to office and – after the war – Greece reaped the rewards of its new alliance when it received a grant of territory in Turkey, Germany's beaten ally.

However, Alexander's brief reign ended in tragedy when he was bitten by his pet monkey and died of blood poisoning. Prince George was passed over once again, and this time Venizelos offered the Crown to the late King's younger brother, Prince Paul. The offer was firmly declined. Soon after, Venizelos was thrown out in an election and, after a plebiscite, King Constantine was recalled from exile. But his triumph was short-lived. Two years later – in the wake of defeat in the Graeco–Turkish War of 1921–2 – he was again forced to leave his throne. He died in exile the following year.

Meanwhile, as Prince Philip sailed off in his orange-box, Constantine's eldest son, George, had finally made it to the throne as George II. In the turbulent state of Greek politics, though, he soon lost his grip on power. In 1923, after a reign lasting only a year, he too was forced into exile – going first to Romania, the home of his wife Queen Elizabeth. Later he spent time in London and Florence before being restored to his throne in 1935 by the Right-wing General Kondylis – who had taken over from Pangalos after a *coup d'etat* 10 years before. However, within 12 months the King felt sufficiently sure of his position to engineer a *coup* which dismissed Kondylis and installed in his place the dictator Metaxas. To confirm the re-establishment of the monarchy, George II then had the bodies of his father and mother and his grandmother Queen Olga exhumed for reburial in Greece. The coffins were brought to Athens from the Florence cemetery where the exiles had been buried, and were laid in state for six days before being ceremoniously interred in the royal burial ground. In fact, the event was something of a family reunion festival, and among the guests was Prince Philip – by this time a Danish national thanks to King Christian x. All the kith and kin of the royal clan rode through flag-bedecked streets and cheering crowds. They were so numerous that they occupied the whole of the *Grande Bretagne*, the finest hotel in Athens.

Three years later, the family was celebrating again. This time it was the marriage of the King's brother Prince Paul to Frederika of Brunswick. As the bride was a member of the Guelph House of Hanover, she was governed by the Royal Marriage Act of 1772 and required the consent of the head of the family, King George VI of Great Britain.

The Court Circular in London duly carried notification of the King's consent. At the wedding itself, Prince Philip – again among those present – played a prominent though essentially functionless role. During the ceremony he had to stand behind the bride and groom while his cousins, King Michael of Romania and David Mountbatten, held the golden crowns over their heads as required by the rite of the Greek Orthodox Church. The event went off without a hitch, which is more than could be said for the formal display of the wedding presents afterwards. When he was inspecting a serviceable pair of silver vegetable dishes, Frederika's Uncle Jakob started back and turned to the Duke of Kent, whose marriage to Princess Marina of Greece had taken place just four years before. 'Hallo!' said the angry uncle, 'What's this? These are the dishes I gave you and Marina for your wedding.'

Two years later, on 28 October 1940, Italy invaded Greece. The Royal Navy was already badly overstretched in the Mediterranean and its bases at Malta and Alexandria were under heavy attack, but it convoyed what supplies it could to British troops in the Greek Islands. Prince Philip was a junior officer on HMS *Valiant*, one of the convoy ships, and he managed to snatch a fleeting visit to Athens in the spring of 1941. There, he found King George and Queen Elizabeth, Prince Paul and Frederika and his own mother Princess Alice in high good humour at the Greek army's respectable showing in the war. He watched an air-raid with them from the roof of the palace, and impressed one and all with his professional comments on the enemy action. However, after a couple of days he was off again – this time to get himself mentioned in despatches at the Battle of Cape Matapan, when the Royal Navy scored a big success over the Italian Fleet.

On 6 April 1941, German armies invaded from Bulgaria. Although King George declared the determination of the country to continue the fight, he and the government knew they faced almost certain defeat. After several sleepless days and nights had drained 'every vestige of colour from his face and made his hands shake as he held a cup and saucer', the King and his family finally took flight. They reassembled in Alexandria, and there – joined by cousin Philip – passed a few hectic happy days. King George later went to London where, like many of Europe's war-exiled monarchs, he enjoyed the hospitality of his cousin, George VI.

Meanwhile in Greece the Germans and their puppet governments faced dogged resistance, despite ruthless reprisals. However, even while the guerillas controlled large areas of the country they were at odds between themselves. As early as 1943, sporadic fighting broke out between communist ELAS and royalist EDES groups. When the British drove the last German troops out of the country in September 1944, the sectarian fighting became widespread. As the Civil War gained momentum, the King awaited the decision of his people about his future. A plebiscite held in September 1946, decided for his return, but in the following year communists set up a rival government in the

Above far left, *the Greek king, George II, shortly before his abdication in 1923.* Centre far left, *King George and President Roosevelt during a wartime visit to America.* Below far left, *George of Greece with King Peter of Yugoslavia at a wartime reception in London held to celebrate the signing of a pact between their governments in exile.* Left, *an informal pose taken after his restoration in 1935.*

often went into the mountains in the wake of the army to bring back children orphaned in the fighting or abandoned by parents who had joined the guerillas. She loved dancing with the peasants in village squares – being jostled by the crowds eager to see and touch her; or pushing through the communist lines with troops going to beleaguered towns. Of course Frederika believed she had good reason to hate and fear communism. Her brother, Prince Ernest Augustus, had once been interned as a prisoner-of-war with a group of communists. Later he told his sister that they had got on well enough, but he had been told that, 'After the war, your lot will be the first to have your throats cut.'

The Greek Civil War continued with outstanding viciousness and brutality on both sides. However, King Paul's government – run by the (royalist) Populist Party – was widely criticized for the economic stringency of the times, for its restrictions on political freedoms, and for its general incompetence. Nevertheless, by 1950 the communist threat had been largely contained, and some sort of stability had at last returned to the war-torn country. In June 1952, King Paul and Queen Frederika made a State Visit to Turkey . . . and even visited Istanbul (formerly Constantinople). This was indeed a dramatic gesture, since tradition held that no Greek ruler should set foot, except as a conqueror, in the city which, centuries before, had been the capital of the Greek Christian Empire. But hatchets were being buried in all directions, for in 1954 Greece not only signed an alliance with Turkey, but also one with communist Yugoslavia, while the King and Queen even exchanged visits with President Tito.

Under King Paul and his long-serving Prime Minister Karamanlis, though, Greece was firmly allied with the Western world and liked to present itself as essentially liberal. When the old King died in March 1964, he was succeeded by his 24-year-old son, Constantine II. In July 1965, Constantine ousted the left-wing administration of Papandreou, and was immediately accused by many Greeks of being too greatly attentive to his mother's wishes. She had, her enemies claimed, near-Nazi sentiments. However, a succession of ministries followed, and Constantine announced his plans for elections to be held in May 1967. But his plans were forestalled by a military *coup* on 21 April, when the notorious regime of the Colonels began. In December, the King's attempt at a counter-*coup* failed miserably, and with

mountains to the north. They claimed support from Bulgaria and Yugoslavia; whereas the royalists were strongly supported by Britain and the USA. However, King George died in 1947, and was succeeded by his brother Paul and his forceful and passionately anti-communist Queen, Frederika.

Educated at an English boarding school, Frederika was – by her own report – a vigorous subversive of the established order there. She led protests against the petty regulations of the place, and in her memoirs even claims to have forced the authorities to drop cricket in favour of lacrosse. She spent much of her wartime exile in South Africa and, in 1941, toured Cape Province with her cousin Philip who had managed to get himself a few days' shore-leave.

So when Prince Paul came to the throne, 'Freddie' predictably threw all her considerable energies into the fight against communist insurgents. In July 1947 the Royal Welfare Institute was founded, with most of the finance supplied by the Queen's enthusiastic American female volunteers. In Frederika's words: 'It was a home for the rescue of children from the communists.' She and her numerous helpers

monarchy. In the campaign that followed, the King's supporters proposed his attempted counter-*coup* of 1967 as evidence of his democratic credentials, and even announced that his mother should not return if he was restored. It was all in vain, and the vote in December 1974 returned a majority of seven-to-three in favour of retaining the republic. This time the monarch accepted the decision of his people as a true expression of their views. It is difficult to imagine the circumstances in which the latest of Greece's exiled Kings, could continue the special tradition of his family and make a comeback.

The last three generations of the Greek royal house. Above far left, King Paul at an official review. Below left, with Queen Frederika during the civil war period, at a review of royalist troops in their headquarters at Lamia, 22 May 1948. Above left, a royal christening. The young Constantine and Anne Marie of Greece pose with their parents, Queen Ingrid of Denmark, Queen Frederika and King Frederick IX of Denmark. Below, King Constantine of the Hellenes, in full dress uniform, takes the salute.

that he went into exile in Rome. 'I am sure,' he said, 'I shall go back the way my ancestors did.'

Certainly the precedents must have seemed promising, but the world – and even Greece – has changed a great deal since the monarchy made its most recent comeback. Then, Constantine himself seemed a modern young man. He had begun his education in a special palace school planned by his father and attended by nine other boys, carefully selected from varied social backgrounds. From there he went to boarding school, military academy and Athens University. He proved a world-class sportsman, making the Greek Olympic sailing team and gaining a black belt in karate. In 1964, he married Princess Anne Marie of Denmark – a person with impeccable democratic credentials. In Greece, though, even such a 'modern' monarchy was still too involved in the government process to have a chance of developing his rule on the constitutionally neutral lines of the northern European kingdoms. As a result, the Greeks' decision to remove their King in 1967 was forced on them though it may have seemed this time to have been a vote for a true change of system and a complete break.

Nevertheless, Constantine continued to watch events in his country from his exile with his family in a comfortable villa on the outskirts of Rome. In June 1973, he heard George Papadopoulos, the Colonels' leader, condemn him as 'a collaborator with foreign forces and with murderers', and accuse him of 'pursuing ambitions to become a political leader'. It was soon clear that, stripped of its abuse, the statement had a factual basis. A few days before some Greek navy officers had attempted a *coup* with royalist leanings which failed. There followed a 'popular' plebiscite under the aegis of the regime, which showed that 78% of the voters were in favour of a republic. Not surprisingly, the King refused to accept such a verdict. But in November, Papadopoulos was ousted in his turn. The following year, Karamanlis was recalled to head Greek affairs, and Constantine confidently awaited an invitation to return. However, none was issued, although Constantine publicly welcomed the developments at home and made formal visits to Buckingham Palace and 10 Downing Street from his new house in London. Then, to Constantine's intense disappointment, Karamanlis decided to hold a referendum on the issue of the

Democratic Monarchs

Whereas monarchy in southern Europe has left hectic and colourful chronicles, in the north it has proved more enduring, perhaps because it has been more circumspect. In fact, it seems doubtful whether the baubled autocrats of the past would even have recognized as kings many of those who now wear their crowns. Yet, for a variety of reasons, a cluster of countries still find themselves more comfortable with a King rather than a President as their Head of State.

In Norway and Sweden – peopled by descendants of the warlike Vikings – the monarchs have been disciplined to the gentle, homely style of senior bureaucrats.

On one famous occasion, for instance, the ageing King Haakon of Norway was drenched to the skin while conducting an open-air review at Stavanger in 1952. He had an austere sense of kingly duty and, while the officials in the party may have thought differently, he accepted such discomforts phlegmatically. At the end of the day, the little group in the royal hotel room felt that a stiff brandy might be a wise as well as a pleasant precaution. However, Norway's tight licensing laws forbade the consumption of alcohol on the premises. It was a dilemma of constitutional propriety *vs* royal prerogative. Boldly, the King stretched the rules. 'If,' he pronounced, 'the Mayor of Stavanger will open it, the Sheriff pour it out and the Minister of Justice hand it round, I think we may deem it permissible for medicinal purposes.'

If he had known that monarchy would one day conduct itself with such constrained democratic manners, even King John of England would have drowned his sorrows with a happier spirit while affixing his seal to Magna Carta. In fact, since that historic royal humiliation in 1215, a running battle between the Crown and its subjects has formed an intermittent backdrop to English constitutional history. In 1649 King Charles I lost his head; in 1688 King James II lost his throne; and when, in 1834, King William IV dismissed his government, it was described by a contemporary as 'the greatest piece of folly ever committed'. Perhaps with half a mind to this warning, no British monarch has ever dared to do the same again. Yet 'silly Billy' William, whose supporters even said 'cuts a damnable figure', was also responsible for stamp-

ing the British monarchy with its indelible democratic image. Had William had his way, in fact, there would have been no coronation – 'a useless and ill-timed expense' he called it. In the end, however, he had to content himself with a drastic pruning of the traditional pomp and circumstance, to produce what his subjects jeeringly referred to as his 'half-crownation'. Strangely, the English – though vociferous on the subject of their 'liberties' – have always liked glamour from their monarchs.

William gave those liberties a decided boost when, in 1832, he helped his government push through the Great Reform Bill. This was an historic first step towards universal suffrage. The process was completed nearly a century later when, in 1928, the voting qualifications for women were made the same as those for men. However, the King of the day, George V, was old-fashioned in his views and did not much approve of this reform, nor of women MPs. He sent a courtier to express his dismay to the Prime Minister on hearing that during all-night sessions MPs stretched out on the benches for a rest. 'Members of Parliament now include ladies,' ran the message, 'and such a state of things as you describe seems to His Majesty hardly decorous.'

George V, who had come to the throne at the age of 45 in 1910, was distinguished 'by no personal magnetism, by no intellectual powers. He was neither a wit . . . well read nor well educated.' He was, in short, like most of his subjects. Somewhat pompously perhaps, he has been called 'the first British monarch to exemplify the majesty of the ordinary man'. To be sure, few of the ordinary men (or women) of England could share a whisky flask with the Archbishop of Canterbury during a deerstalk in the Scottish Highlands. But then the English – who boast of Westminster as the 'mother of parlia-

ments' – equally expect their King to be 'a real gentleman'. On this, King George wholeheartedly agreed. Like his father Edward VII, he was a pedant for protocol and, like his son Edward VII, for correct dress. However, as often happens, the father's and son's views on what constitutes 'correct dress' were widely divergent. One morning, for instance, the young Edward – then Prince of Wales – arrived for breakfast wearing trousers with 'cuffs' in the new American fashion. In his father's world no 'gentleman' turned up his trousers except, perhaps, to cross a puddle. 'Is it raining in *here*?' roared the King.

Such concerns were fitting for the monarch of an aristocratic Court, but King George also had a genuine and deep feeling for the legion of Britain's unemployed. In 1921, he wrote to the Prime Minister, Lloyd George, to say

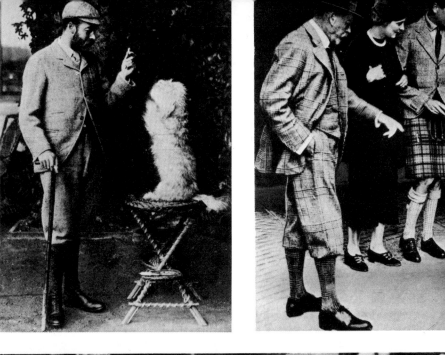

Previous pages, *George V of Great Britain in the year of his accession.* Left, *King George's coronation.* Below, *Prince George and Princess Mary of Wales with their children (1906): Mary, the Princess Royal; Henry, later Duke of Gloucester; George (Duke of Kent); Edward (king as Edward VIII); and George (king as George VI); baby Prince John died aged 14.* Far right, *welcoming George, Duke of Kent and his fiancée, Princess Marina of Greece, at Balmoral.* Centre right, *the King with a favourite pet. Presenting the F.A. cup 1934, to winning Manchester City's captain; King George often attended the Wembley soccer Cup Final.* Below right, *shooting at Sandringham.* Below far right, *at the helm of* Britannia. *George was considered to have a perfect style as a shot and was an excellent helmsman.*

that men wanted work not 'dole' (unemployment benefit) money, and that this money was in any case pitifully inadequate. Then, when a Conservative minority government was defeated in January 1924, the King – 'using (my) own judgement' – sent for Ramsay MacDonald as the leader of the next-largest party, Labour.

This was a truly startling encounter for Britain's supposedly class-ridden society; for MacDonald was not only a socialist, he was also the bastard son of a Scottish peasant farmer. Yet the King came to admire him, and was soon on excellent terms with another Labour minister, J. H. Thomas. George v loved a shady joke – his doctors used to bribe him to take his medicine with the promise of a new one – and 'Jimmy' Thomas had an inexhaustible supply of doubtful humour. Nevertheless, Labour was thrown out that October, in an election dominated by the so-called 'Zinoviev letter'. This was supposedly an intercepted communication from the Kremlin to leading British socialists, and it was predictably hailed by the Right as proof of a near-treacherous conspiracy. However, the King was not convinced of its authenticity and it was, indeed, almost certainly forged.

Despite the turbulent social conditions of the 1920s, George trusted his people. At the time of the General Strike in 1926, Lord Durham – a plutocratic coal-owner – told him that the striking miners were a 'damn lot of revolutionaries'.

'Try living on their wages,' came the gruff royal reply. Clearly the King saw plenty in the state of Britain to justify the anger of the poor. In fact he remonstrated with Churchill – then Chancellor of the Exchequer – for announcing support for the military if they had to suppress the strikers.

After the Strike, Labour came to power for the second time in June 1929. Once again they had no overall majority, and once again the government was overtaken by disaster. By 1931, Europe's financial structure was teetering on the brink of collapse in the shock waves created by America's 'Wall Street Crash' two years before. Financial experts demanded drastic economies to save Sterling, including 10% off the dole. So, at 10 a.m. on Sunday, 23 August, MacDonald went to Buckingham Palace – where the King had arrived barely two hours earlier off the night train from Balmoral – to warn that Labour would probably have to resign. When he left, the King sought advice from the Liberal and Conservative leaders. They advised the formation of a 'national government' under Ramsay MacDonald. Moved by the King's plea that he was 'the man to save the country', the Labour leader eventually concurred although his own Cabinet had already resigned. As a result, the Labour Party saw MacDonald as a traitor, and some even accused the King of collaborating in a plot to split the socialist movement. Certainly, George's part in the affair had been one of the most decisive interventions made by the monarchy in 20th-century British politics. Yet the 'royal prerogative' had been the one constitutional tool left to deal with the crisis. And in urging the Prime Minister to stay on, George had thought to use it in the best interests of the nation.

Throughout his reign George v stolidly aimed to do his duty. Although he was proud to be the King of a 'wonderful people', he was nonetheless fully aware of his own shortcomings and astonished at the tumultuous reception he and Queen Mary received during their Silver Jubilee celebrations in 1935. 'I really think they like me for myself,' he commented. Yet neither he nor Mary were capable of great shows of affection and the majestic and austere figure of the Queen led many people to suppose that she dominated her husband. In fact, the reverse was more likely the case. Young Mary of Teck had been a renowned beauty and, when dresses began to shorten, she looked forward to showing off her shapely legs. First, though, she had to be sure of the King's reaction, so she persuaded one of the ladies to wear the new style at Court. When the King strongly disapproved,

for the rest of her life Mary wore ankle-length dresses which only added to her dominating presence.

Between the wars, Britain was still one of the great powers, and the centre of the world's largest empire. George V was proud of his title of 'King Emperor', and even as he lay dying he was heard to whisper, 'the Empire?' 'It's absolutely all right, Sir,' came the reply of a solicitous courtier. Nevertheless, with the Statute of Westminster in 1935, Canada, Australia, New Zealand and South Africa had already won effective independence as Dominions.

Even at the beginning of George's reign in 1911, a jarring note had been struck at the Royal Durbar in New Delhi. As the King Emperor sat in majesty, receiving the homage of his Indian princes, the Gaekwar of Baroda advanced twirling his cane. During the 1890s the Gaekwar had hobnobbed with the new King's father, Edward VII, at the fashionable German spas, and he may have felt that such casual familiarity was natural between gentlemen. However, King George generally took a less friendly view than his father of his fabulous oriental lieges. When many of them flocked to London during the King's Jubilee year, George V testily demanded: 'Why should they come to London at all and spend a lot of money? Tell them to stay in their states and look after their own subjects.'

In fact this was the same paternalistic concern that George showed for his poorer British subjects. But, as Emperor, he was nonetheless furious at the harassment of his 'loyal officers' by the independence agitations. Once, when he was obliged to receive Mahatma Gandhi, he ended the interview with the words: 'Remember, Mr Gandhi, I won't have any attacks on my Empire.' Tense courtiers no doubt heaved a collective sigh of relief when the little saint suavely replied: 'I must not be drawn into a political argument in your Majesty's palace after receiving your Majesty's hospitality.' In his own way, the King Emperor was probably pleasantly surprised to find that even this 'little man with no proper clothes and bare knees' knew how to behave like 'a gentleman'.

Ordinary almost to a fault, King George V embodied the concept of 'an officer and a gentleman' which the conventional wisdom of Britain then considered the natural quality of a leader. With his grizzled beard, upright carriage and stern but kindly features, he was the image of the ideal *pater familias* – indeed the father-image of a great Imperial family. No doubt this was a sentimental picture but, even in the harsh social conditions endured by most of his subjects, it was one which stirred loyalty, affection and pride in the country. Nor was this monarch a mere wooden Titan impervious to the changing needs and wishes of those he ruled. His people knew him for a good man, and although it was unfashionable in some quarters, the shock of his death in 1936 brought genuine grief into millions of homes. Clement Attlee pronounced a fitting epitaph: 'He was a monarch who knew and understood his people and the age in which they lived, and progressed with them.'

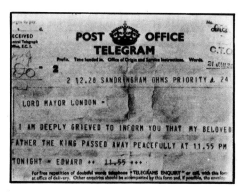

Above from left, *with Albert, King of the Belgians; visiting the war graves, 1922, with Rudyard Kipling; at the Cenotaph service of remembrance – King George's most important annual ceremony; entering St Paul's for the Jubilee service.* Below centre, *George, who initiated the monarch's Christmas broadcasts, giving his last in December 1935.* Left, *Edward VIII's report of his father's death.*

Still more surprising proof of the vitality of monarchy in the 20th century comes from Scandinavia, where Norway presents one of the constitutional mysteries of modern Europe. In 1905, the country had been without a King of its own for half a millenium, but in that year it won its full independence from Sweden. A month later, on 18 November, a junior Prince of the Danish royal house was installed with the title of Haakon VII, King of Norway. To discover why a modern European nation should have marked its independence in this seemingly old-fashioned way calls for a brief excursion into history.

Norway was subject to the Danish Crown from the 14th century down to 1814. In that year, the Danes – allies of the discredited Napoleon Bonaparte – were forced to cede the country to Sweden. For the rest of the century – though Norway was allowed its own government, armed forces and civil service – foreign affairs were retained in the hands of the King of Norway and Sweden. Despite the theory of united kingdoms, during this period most Swedes looked on Norway as a mere province. Then, in 1885, Norwegians became incensed when Swedish foreign affairs were put in the charge of a Council of State. This meant that the King – though excluded from his own country's foreign affairs – remained in charge of Norway's.

Norwegian nationalist agitation concentrated on the demand for separate Norwegian consuls to represent the country's interests abroad. The most powerful voice in the debate was that of Fridtjof Nansen, the renowned Arctic explorer and scientist. One of the greatest figures in contemporary Europe, he brought the Norwegian case international respect. Nevertheless, the Swedish royal government remained adamant. So, in 1905, the Norwegian government resigned, and King Oscar 'of Norway and Sweden' could find no politician willing to form a new one. The Storting (parliament) accordingly resolved that since there was no royal government, the constitutional royal power was in abeyance. It then empowered the resigning administration to 'exercise the power granted to the King ... subject to the changes made necessary by the fact that the union between Sweden and Norway under the said King is dissolved.' That day, as he watched the members stream out of the Storting building, *The Times* correspondent observed to a Danish journalist: 'Quite a gentlemanly revolution, isn't it?' But it *was* a revolution nonetheless.

As panic rumours hinted at an impending war between Norway and Sweden, practical politicians sat down to debate the form of the new constitution. Republicanism seemed modern, but was it practical? Switzerland and France apart, Europe was solidly monarchist, and even French statesmen favoured a monarchical regime in Norway. The Norwegian Prime Minister wryly observed that the country would win friends if it introduced a new member to the 'trades union of kings'. Still more to the point, a

Above left, *King Oscar II of Sweden.* Above, *the King opens the Swedish parliament.* Below, *King Haakon VII, Queen Maude and Crown Prince Olaf of Norway.* Below right, *Haakon crowned in Trondheim Cathedral, 22 June 1906; the crown is held over his head as he hears the benediction of the Church.*

'King of Norway' would be a focus of loyalties above the rivalries of political parties in the new state.

But if a King, who should it be? Oscar of Sweden was proving slow to renounce his title, but despite this – and the ill-feeling between the two countries – the Swedish royal house was invited to put up another of its members as a candidate for the new Crown. If the Swedes had been openly snubbed no other European family would have considered accepting, but in the event they did not respond at all. So the possible alternative candidates were soon narrowed down to 47-year-old Prince Valdemar, third son of Christian IX of Denmark, and 33-year-old Prince Carl, Christian's grandson and a nephew of Edward VII – who telegraphed King Oscar not to oppose the candidature. Carl, an officer in the Danish navy, was not only young but he had also had an infant son who could grow up a good Norwegian. The country approved the institution of a new monarchy by referendum and – on 18 November 1905 – the Storting elected Prince Carl of Denmark as King of independent Norway. He received the news while inspecting a torpedo boat in Copenhagen harbour.

In the country at large, the King's new subjects were hardly better prepared. At first, it even looked as though

he would have to make his ceremonial entry in a coach used by his Swedish predecessors. But a coachbuilder was eventually found with a suitably handsome equippage for hire. Although the royal ship docked in driving snow, the auguries for the reign brightened when the three-year-old Crown Prince, now renamed Olaf, relieved his boredom at listening to all the welcoming committee's speeches by seizing a Norwegian flag from a boy at the front of the crowd and waving it lustily.

The new King, who had assumed the title of Haakon VII – a name from the heroic Norse past – was crowned on 22 June 1906. The crown was placed on his head jointly by the Bishop of Bergen and the Prime Minister, while the sceptre, orb and sword of state were presented to the monarch by other ministers. Yet even this democratic ceremony was thought too mystical an inauguration for modern Norway, and early in 1908 the Storting abolished the symbolic act of coronation.

In Sweden, meanwhile, the monarch is no longer referred to even as King, but – in good republican style – as Head of State; while the Dutch monarchy has managed to prosper for over 160 years without the benefit of any sort of religious coronation. In the context of the modern institution such ideas are not unusual. However, the English – famed

for their illogicality – are unlikely ever to pledge their loyalty to an uncrowned King. For them, the ceremony is a high moment of national dedication. As George VI remembered on the day of his coronation: 'I could eat no breakfast and had a sinking feeling inside.'

George had, however, been viewing the approaching ceremony for months with trepidation. In fact, as he and Lord Louis Mountbatten stood watching his elder brother packing his things after his abdication, George turned to his cousin with the words: 'But Dickie, this is quite terrible. I don't know how to be a King; the only thing I've ever been trained for is the navy.' George V had addressed virtually the same words to Mountbatten's father on hearing of the death of his elder brother in 1895. 'I will give you the reply my father gave yours,' said Dickie Mountbatten. 'A King could not have a better training than the navy.'

Prince Albert George, 'Bertie' to the family, had been a sickly baby who grew up to be a gawky boy. He was forced to wear splints to cure his knock-knees and, although naturally left-handed, he was dragooned into writing with his right. It is hardly surprising that when he was about seven he began to show signs of a stammer, which soon developed into an appalling stutter. His dismal record continued when he was sent to the naval academy at Dartmouth. 'Mr Johnson', as he was called, was treated with almost exaggerated disregard for his rank, and was prominent only at the bottom of the table of exam results.

However, the Prince did see action. On 31 May 1916, sub-lieutenant Johnson was part of the crew of 'A' turret on HMS *Collingwood* in the Battle of Jutland. No one doubted his courage or his determination, but illhealth soon put an end to his naval career. After convalescing from an operation for an ulcer, he joined the Royal Naval Air Service at Cranwell, where he was put in charge of the boy cadets. With characteristic thoroughness he decided that he should know how to fly. Although he did not enjoy it, he doggedly pushed ahead with the course and eventually passed. Nowadays, one of the few features of the British monarchy to have survived the brief, disastrous reign of Edward VIII is the Household Air Squadron or 'Royal Flight' – just the sort of 'modern' thing one would expect of the dynamic and glamorous Edward. However, not he but his plodding brother was the first British monarch to be a qualified pilot.

Bertie brought similar determination to his courtship of the Lady Elizabeth

Bowes-Lyon, pressing his suit despite early refusals. Their marriage in 1923 was the best thing that ever happened to him. Lady Elizabeth was beautiful, sparkling and quick-witted, and she had a warmth and approachability that would compensate in their public life together for his diffidence. When, as the Duke and Duchess of York, they returned after a triumphant Commonwealth tour in 1927, it was obvious that the British royal family had acquired a dedicated new team.

By this time, even Bertie's stutter was yielding to treatment, just as the Prince had begun to despair. In October 1926, only weeks before the tour, he had responded to his wife's urgent pleadings and kept an appointment with an Australian speech therapist, Lionel Logue. Within days, Logue's course of breathing exercises and encouragement showed results. Afterwards,

---

Left, *King George VI at Buckingham Palace.* Above, *King George V with his sons in Windsor Great Park.* Right, *a honeymoon picture of the Duke and Duchess of York, 1923.*

Bertie was always liable to find his handicap waiting in ambush at times of crisis, but he had mastered it to the extent that he was able to continue the traditional Christmas radio broadcasts to the Empire begun by his father.

The traumatic sequence of events that brought George VI to the throne has already been recounted. In the event, he went to his coronation on the day planned for his brother's, and the omens were alternately worrying and absurd. For instance, in preparation for the trendy Edward, souvenir manufacturers had turned out a startling range of oddities including women's corsets embellished on the hip with a crown flanked by a lion and a unicorn. Then, during the actual ceremony, the Crown of St Edward was at first lowered onto the King's head back-to-front; while a bishop – inadvertently standing on the King's train – almost brought him down. 'I had to tell him off pretty sharply,' George noted later in his diary.

In the meantime, of course, Europe was moving towards war. When the King offered to appeal directly to the Axis leaders as Head of State, he was turned down by the government for fear he would meet with rebuff. It was a bitter lesson in the restricted role of a modern democratic monarch. So, when war came, the royal family played the one role open to them with unassuming steadiness and courage – living through the Blitz with the rest of the country, and visiting the bombed disaster areas of the capital of other towns. Once, after a raid on the East End of London, a survivor called out: 'Thank God for a good King.' Emotionally, the King replied: 'And thank God for a good people.' Ironically, a daring *Luftwaffe* pilot cemented the bond of loyalty between King and people. Flying low down the length of the Mall, he roared close over the roofs of Buckingham Palace and unloaded a cluster of bombs. One stick fell directly outside the window where the King was working, and others wrecked the chapel. When they had recovered from the shock, the royal family welcomed their baptism by fire. 'It makes me feel,' commented the Queen, 'I can look the East End in the face.'

In 1939–40, some wealthy British families were leaving for America, or at least sending their children there ... but the royal family did no such thing. As the Queen said: 'The children cannot go without me and I will not leave the King, and the King of course will not go.' George, who had always been the best shot in a family of sportsmen, now took daily revolver and rifle practice in the grounds of Buckingham Palace. He planned to lead the resistance forces if invasion came.

Thanks in large part to a conscientious sense of duty, George VI and Elizabeth triumphantly continued the gradual democratization of the monarchy begun by George V. A good 'desk monarch', Bertie made careful notes on his meetings with his ministers, and he insisted that all letters should be seen by himself before they went to his private secretary. He even earned the respect of Winston Churchill, a fierce partisan of Edward VIII during the abdication crisis. When the Allies launched their attack on Nazi-occupied Europe in June 1944, the great wartime Prime Minister ardently wished to visit the beach-heads. However, he did not go because the King insisted that he would go along as well. Clement Attlee, the Labour Prime Minister, also learned to respect the King's qualities. When he surprised the pundits by appointing Ernest Bevin to the foreign office, it was partly in deference to the King's shrewd advice. Like most kings, George placed a high value on foreign affairs. He not only thought Bevin the best-qualified person for the job, but he also got on well with him. At the time there were many people in America as well as Britain who accused George of 'demanding' that Bevin be given the appointment. In fact he merely 'begged' the Prime Minister 'to think carefully', and suggested that 'Mr Bevin would be the better choice'.

King George VI knew his place as a constitutional monarch too well to 'demand' anything. Yet he retained firm ideas about the dignity of kings. When it was suggested that he should go into hospital for one of his operations, he replied: 'I never heard of a king going into hospital before.' Clearly, he also entertained doubts about the future of the monarchy in Britain. On one occasion, when he learned from the heiress of an ancient landed family that the family home would have to be sold to the National Trust, he commented sadly: 'Everything is going nowadays. Before long, I also shall have to go.'

Above left, *in the streets of war-torn London, September 1940.* Below left, *at a reception (London, February 1940) for relatives of sailors lost during the naval victory of the River Plate.* Below, *George VI driving back to Sandringham after bidding farewell to Princess Elizabeth at London Airport, 31 January 1952. He died a week later.*

H.M. Queen Elizabeth II

Queen Elizabeth II was born on 21 April 1926, at 17 Bruton Street, London – the home of her mother, Elizabeth Duchess of York. She was named Elizabeth Alexandra Mary, after her mother, grandmother and great-grandmother respectively. In something of a break with tradition for girls of her House, there was, in the words of King George V: 'Nothing about Victoria.' Nevertheless, the King approved the choice although later he dubbed her 'Lilibet', from her early attempts to pronounce her own name.

Ever since she had consented to marry 'Bertie' – the family name for the future George VI – the beautiful and sparkling Elizabeth, Duchess of York, had quickly become a favourite with the old King. This new Elizabeth soon found equal favour. Queen Marie of Romania, a cousin of George V, once said: 'My English family was and is terribly exclusive, and only grudgingly opens its doors to strangers.' Within that family circle though, the little newcomer was surrounded by love. 'We always wanted a child,' wrote her father, 'to make our happiness complete. Now that it has happened, it seems so wonderful and strange.'

From the first, Elizabeth shaped up to become a lively and practical little girl. One Christmas, a present of a housemaid's set – complete with dustpan and brush – provoked in her a 'passion for housework' that hinted at the near-obsession with tidiness and order that later became part of her childhood. Like many girls of her class, she soon developed an engrossing enthusiasm for pony-riding, and today she is a horsewoman of competition calibre. In August 1930, Elizabeth was joined in the nursery by a sister. Mischievous and vivacious, Princess Margaret Rose was to be more than a little spoilt by her father. For her part, Elizabeth had the same prim sense of responsibility that many little girls show for a younger sister. Later, when the great day of their parents' coronation was approaching, she enquired pensively about Margaret:

'She's very young for a coronation, isn't she?'

Her uncle Edward VIII's abdication was the first cloud on the edge of Elizabeth's life. However, she faced it matter-of-factly; a note she wrote that day was dated simply 'Abdication Day'. Although it was a day that re-shaped her future and made her father and mother the King and Queen of England, in the meanwhile the happy days of a privileged life rolled on. However, the family had to leave their home at 145 Piccadilly, Hyde Park Corner, for Buckingham Palace, and the wonderful visits to Glamis Castle – her mother's family home in Scotland – became less frequent in favour of the royal residence at Balmoral. The children did not take to the London palace. Its vast rooms and rambling corridors seemed so unfriendly. 'People here need bicycles,' Elizabeth observed.

Even so, life in a palace proved not to be so bad after all. At Christmas, she and Margaret mounted pantomimes and plays with their friends; both loved acting and both had – and still have – a natural gift for mimicry. When the war came and the portraits were removed to safety, Margaret found the frames ideally suited for posters advertising the forthcoming production of *Mother Goose*. 'How do you like my ancestors?' the King would then ask of his guests. But Elizabeth, by this time in her teens, thought she should be doing more for the war-effort than merely sharing the Blitz with the Londoners, or living in

the comparative safety of Windsor Castle with the family. So, in 1945, after constant urging, her father eventually allowed her to do her National Service, and Second Lieutenant Elizabeth Windsor – of the Auxilliary Transport Service, Mechanical Transport Training Centre No 1 – was soon to be photographed wielding a spanner. By this time she was already a good driver, quite capable of changing a wheel and doing simple repairs.

The year before, Elizabeth had reached the age of 18 – the traditional age of majority for royalty. Some thought that, as heir to the throne, she should be created Princess of Wales. But her father, a stickler for convention, rejected the suggestion and convinced the Cabinet that the title was exclusively the entitlement of the wife of a Prince of Wales. For her part, his daughter was contemplating a far more significant change of status. Romance had entered her life. Philip, the dashing young naval officer we have already seen adventuring in the Mediterranean, had been an occasional visitor at Windsor Castle since 1943. Private talks about an engagement hardened into agreement between the young people during Philip's summer visit to Balmoral in 1946. At first the King was reluctant for his daughter to leave home, but the Princess had made up her mind. Philip spent that Christmas with the royal family at Sandringham, and in February his long-standing application for British citizenship at last went

through. Still King George wished the official announcement to be postponed, and in the spring Elizabeth accompanied her parents on a tour of South Africa.

At last, in July 1947, the announcement came from Buckingham Palace of the betrothal of the King and Queen's 'dearly beloved daughter, the Princess Elizabeth, to Lieutenant Philip Mountbatten, RN, son of the late Prince Andrew of Greece and Princess Andrew (Princess Alice of Battenberg), to which union the King has gladly given his consent.' The wedding took place later that year, on 20 November. The pomp and splendour of the ceremony made a glittering display in the austerity of post-war Britain. Costly presents flooded in from all parts of the world, but among those most treasured was a simple table mat. This was the gift of Mahatma Gandhi, who had spun the thread on his own spinning-wheel and had it woven up to his own design.

The wedding was followed by a honeymoon, which was unhappily disturbed by press intrusions and bus-loads of sightseers ferried out from London to the Mountbatten's country estate at Broadlands. In fact for the next four years the young couple had to fight a running battle with press and protocol to live something approaching a normal life. Prince Philip, in particular, was dourly determined to live his own life and continue his career as a naval officer before the dreaded descent of what he called 'the royal rigmarole'. Suitably accoutred with royal titles – His Royal Highness, Baron Greenwich, Earl of Merioneth and Duke of Edinburgh, Knight of the Garter (eight days his wife's junior in the Order) – Philip also received a taxed salary of £10,000 from Parliament to fit him for the ceremonial life. But at least as valuable as all these 'perks' to the 26-

With father, mother and sister. Far left, leaving St Paul's after the service of thanksgiving for King George V's jubilee. Left, at the Royal Lodge, Windsor, 1940. Below, with the family and her fiancé.

year-old junior officer, was the order from his superiors to take the Naval Staff Course at Greenwich – necessary if he was to receive senior commissions.

Then, in November 1948, King George suffered a sudden and serious illness and Lilibet and her husband suddenly found themselves in the front line of official duties. Many, including his doctors, thought the King's illness would be his last. Instead, he made a surprising recovery. In July 1949, his daughter and her husband moved into the beautiful London home, Clarence House, which he had given them. And in October they were off to Malta for Philip to take up a commission as First Lieutenant in HMS *Chequers*.

Those were happy years. The birth of Prince Charles, on 14 November 1948, had meant a renewed burst of popularity for the royal pair, and the months they spent in Malta were as near the life of private citizens as they were ever likely to experience. Philip's commission, and his new enthusiasm for polo – at which he soon proved expert – fitted his wish for a full naval career. Although she was always guest of honour at any function they attended, and she did her fair share of 'the royal rigmarole', Elizabeth – beautiful and in love – nonetheless enjoyed to the full her position as a young bride in the world of privilege. In the summer of 1950, she returned to England for the birth of her second child, Princess Anne, on 15 August. The next month, Philip was commissioned as commander of the frigate HMS *Magpie*. He drove his men almost as hard as he drove himself – winning their respect, though hardly their affection.

The commander of HMS *Magpie* and his wife were sent on a series of semi-official State Visits to Gibraltar, Cyprus, Egypt and elsewhere. However, their most pleasant trip was to visit King Paul and Queen Frederika in Athens in the early summer of 1951. After that happy family occasion, though, it was back to business. In October, Philip and Elizabeth flew to Canada for an exhausting public schedule of 14- and 16-hour days. The reception they received wherever they went was wildly enthusiastic and, when they made a brief excursion across the border to pay a State Visit to President Truman, crowds estimated at 500,000 turned out to greet them in Washington.

The following January, this much-travelled couple boarded a flight for Nairobi, Kenya, on the first leg of a Commonwealth Tour which was to take them on to Australia and New Zealand. On Wednesday, 5 February, they

checked in at *Treetops Hotel*, which is a little four-room house built in a huge fig tree, overlooking a waterhole in a clearing in the Kenyan forest. They were both enchanted, and the Princess shot some marvellous film footage of animals feeding at the waterhole. The following afternoon, as he was having a siesta, Philip was awakened by his secretary with the news that King George VI had died that morning.

The young woman in her mid-20s, now Queen, heard the news from her husband after he – disbelieving at first – had got confirmation from London. She bore the blow, heavy and unexpected as it was, with cool fortitude. The royal party, busy with preparations for the return to London, had little time to feel the full weight of mourning for a beloved King or pride that their young mistress was now their monarch. Just 24 hours later, Elizabeth was descending the steps of the blue-and-silver airliner *Atalanta,* to be received as Queen by a welcoming party waiting in the sombre black of mourning on the tarmac of London Airport. Among the dignitaries was Winston Churchill, once again Prime Minister, and his predecessor, Earl Attlee. After a few words with them, Elizabeth was driven to Buckingham Palace. On the morning of Friday, 8 February, Queen Elizabeth II held her Accession Council in St James's Palace – the first official act of her reign. Only then did she make her way to Sandringham where the old King lay, and where her mother and sister awaited her.

Elizabeth came to the throne as the last monarch of the House of Windsor. Her children bore the name of her husband, and Prince Charles – when he in turn should become King – would inaugurate the House of Mountbatten. That was the normal course of events, and so it remained from 6 February to 9 April, 1952. On that day, bitterly against her will, the Queen – in the age-old formula – proclaimed as her 'Will and Pleasure that She and Her Children shall be styled and known as the House and Family of Windsor, and that Her descendants, other than female descendants who marry, and their descendants shall bear the name of Windsor.' It was, perhaps, natural enough for the nation to wish to preserve the name of Windsor for its ruling dynasty. However, the removal of the name of Mountbatten from the title was an affront to a family which had served Britain long, loyally and well.

As First Sea Lord, Prince Louis of Battenberg – Philip's grandfather – had decisively improved Britain's chances of naval preparedness when, on his own

initiative in July 1914, he halted the dispersal of the Third Fleet back to its bases. As a result, when World War I broke out the following month, the British warships in the North Sea could move smoothly into action. Yet before the year was out, Prince Louis had been forced to resign by a popular upsurge of anti-German feeling which clearly extended to those German princes close to the royal family. The Battenbergs duly anglicized their name to Mountbatten, and even the royal family – named either Guelph, or Wettin or possibly Coburg, but at any rate something German – felt compelled to change its style to that of 'the House of Windsor'. King George V, who deplored the hysterical clamour, was not happy. The Kaiser, reasonably enough, was drily amused. 'I look forward,' he observed on hearing the news from England, 'to attending the next performance of *The Merry Wives of Saxe–Coburg–Gotha.*'

So, in April, 1952 – nearly half a century later – the English were to change their royal family's name yet again. This time it was not merely to retain the name of Windsor, but also to drop the name of Mountbatten altogether. For years the conservative Beaverbrook newspapers had waged a vendetta against the family, and there were also some at Court who disliked (or envied) those they considered 'pushy upstarts'. However, many in the country – not least the Prime Minister Winston Churchill – disliked the part which, as Viceroy of India, Lord Louis

Far left, *a christening photograph of Prince Charles, December 1948.* Left, *George VI with Queen Elizabeth and their grandchildren, Charles and Anne.* Below, *7 February 1952. HM Queen Elizabeth II leaving the airliner which had flown her back to Britain from Kenya on the news of her father's death. Winston Churchill awaits her.*

Mountbatten had played in the dissolution of Britain's Empire there. Under this heavy nationalistic pressure, and despite her love for her husband, Elizabeth at last bowed to her Prime Minister's 'formal and insistent advice' . . . and signed the Order for the change of name.

Needless to say, the Queen resented the slight. In September another Royal Warrant ordained that 'HRH Philip, Duke of Edinburgh, henceforth and on all occasions . . . have, hold and enjoy Place, Pre-eminence, and Precedent next to her Majesty'. Before this Order, Philip had ranked behind the royal dukes and even behind his own children. When he returned from a long and successful Commonwealth Tour in 1957, the Queen demonstrated her feelings about yet another press campaign against the Duke – which even suggested that he had delayed his return because of a rift between them – by creating him a Prince of the United Kingdom. Finally, on 8 February 1960, she declared in Council that her descendants should bear the name Mountbatten-Windsor. 'The Queen,' ran an explanatory statement, 'has had this in mind for a long time and it is close to her heart.' On her wedding day – 14 November 1973 – Princess Anne was to sign her name in the register of Westminster Abbey as 'Anne Mountbatten-Windsor'.

Even before she came to the throne, in a broadcast on her 21st birthday, Elizabeth had dedicated her life to her people. 'I declare,' she said, 'before you all that my whole life, whether it be long or short, shall be devoted to your service and the service of our great Imperial family to which we all belong . . . God help me to make good my vow, and God bless all of you who are willing to share it.' Of course that duty began in earnest the day she returned to England from Kenya, when she first opened the boxes containing the state papers her father had been working on. If application to paperwork is the mark of a devoted monarch, Queen Elizabeth II has certainly fulfilled her vow. Incredibly, only hours after the birth of Prince Andrew on 19 February, 1960, his mother – propped up on her pillows – was already back at her reading. Over the years, her prime ministers have consistently paid tribute to her excellent briefing on political affairs. In particular, Sir Harold Wilson recalled that what he had supposed would be a pleasant and purely formal break from

his ministerial duties, in fact turned out to be a testing weekly interview. A prime minister who had not done his 'homework' thoroughly was liable to find the monarch referring to documents that he had not had time to read, so that he would retire from his audience feeling 'like a naughty schoolboy'. The Queen is known to have a remarkable memory and, in the words of Sir Harold Macmillan: 'Is astonishingly well informed on every detail.'

However, Elizabeth II is a great deal more than just a successful and diligent career woman. From her early 20s, people who knew her began to compare her with her great ancestor Queen Victoria. She has had critics too who might agree with the assessment, considering her either stuffy or conventional. Whether that would be a bad thing might be argued by members of her entourage. But as one Palace official told the Queen's biographer, Robert Lacey: 'Our capital is stuffiness. We don't exist to divert or convert people. We are.' One hopes that the Queen agrees with the sentiment. It is indeed a truly royal statement about monarchy, and one which perhaps could be made only in Buckingham Palace, of all the world's royal residences.

The 'Victorian' aspects of Elizabeth II, as her admirers see the case, are her seriousness of purpose, her dedication, 'the carriage of her head and . . . that indescribable something'. It is perhaps no bad thing in Britain today if there is at the head of affairs at least one person who can be credited with high seriousness. Interestingly, a popular opinion poll in 1969 showed that out of 10 well-known personalities the Duke of Edinburgh was thought likely to make the best dictator . . . and his wife the worst. Whatever that 'indescribable something' is, it is not perceived by her subjects as a dictatorial quality. However, that austere socialist and opponent of monarchy, Sir Stafford Cripps, was in no doubt as to his future monarch's most outstanding quality. In 1947, he said: 'This country is fortunate to have as future Head of State someone with such manifestly good judgement.'

The extent to which the nation as a whole recognized its good fortune was joyfully proclaimed on the day of the Queen's coronation, 2 June 1953. Fittingly for an English early summer's day, the sky was overcast after a night of drizzle and rain. Nevertheless, many among the throng that packed the streets for a glimpse of the Queen in her glorious coach had camped out under the hostile skies all night; many others had travelled from all parts of the

country. Millions more in Britain and throughout the world tuned in to watch the televised coronation.

The great event about to unfold had been prepared for by almost a year's work of the Coronation Commission. The Duke of Norfolk, hereditary Earl Marshall, was in overall charge, while the Queen's consort was chairman. Philip put energy and thoroughness into the work. His already extensive travels around the Commonwealth gave him an authoritative voice in deciding on the details of the participation of its Heads of State; his careful research into the traditions of coronation made him a valuable colleague to the Earl Marshall; and his personal knowledge of the Queen's wishes made her privy to the planning at every stage. Moreover, the Queen insisted on careful rehearsals for the big day. In December 1952, the Commonwealth Conference had settled on a mutually acceptable style for the Queen's title, with a common element for all: 'Queen of Her other Realms and Territories and Head of the Commonwealth'. From the start, Elizabeth was most serious about her role as the figurehead of the largest association of peoples the world has ever seen under a single Crown. Her coronation might be held in the ancient capital of her most ancient Kingdom, but in her own mind her oath was taken to all the peoples who acknowledged her sway.

Inevitably, though, the people of the

United Kingdom felt it was 'their day'. Old Sir Winston Churchill saw in the beautiful young monarch 'the young and gleaming champion'; while Aneurin Bevan – a passionate socialist and architect of the National Health Service – wore his blue lounge suit among the dignitaries in formal dress, but attended cheerfully nevertheless. In the streets, people cheered with almost embarrassed emotion; while in the Abbey all was kind hearts and coronets. News of the successful ascent of Mount Everest by Edmund Hilary and Tensing for the British expedition led by John Hunt was made public, and on every hand journalists and political leaders were to be heard heralding the birth of a new 'Elizabethan Age'. They can be forgiven. She was a lovely Queen, who had truly won her people's hearts. Even the staid *Sociological Review* succumbed: 'The coronation,' ran an article in its December issue, 'provided at one time, and for practically the entire society, such an intensive contact with the sacred that we believe we are justified in interpreting it as a great act of national communion.'

The euphoria did not last. A shadow was cast even over coronation year by the death of old Queen Mary who, in the words of the Countess of Longford, had 'given a protective venerability to the House of Windsor'. In November, Queen Elizabeth and her consort embarked on an immensely successful Commonwealth Tour which seemed to

God Save the Queen

carry forward the high hopes of the coronation. And there were enchanted moments for the Queen herself. As she and her husband were watching a particularly exuberant ceremony of welcome in one of the African territories, she turned to Philip with the words: 'I feel like an African queen.' 'You are an African queen,' he reminded his delighted wife. Even so, there were several occasions on which the Prince allowed his irritation with the crowding reporters to burst out in bad-tempered rudeness. This presaged many storms between the Prince and the press in the coming years. At the time, though, a much more serious press story was already brewing and its ramifications were extensive.

In April, 1953, Princess Margaret had informed her sister that she wished to marry Group Captain Peter Townsend, a favourite equerry of King George VI who was still on the Queen's staff. Handsome, honourable and competent in his duties, Townsend had only one flaw – he had been involved in a divorce case. It is hardly surprising, in view of the cause of Edward VIII's tragedy, that the Princess's romance should have exercised the concern of palace, press and public alike. Many felt that Margaret should have the right to marry whom she would. The Queen, sincerely convinced as to the sanctity of marriage, recognized that should her sister renounce her royal prerogatives, and

anxious for her happiness, then there could be no obstruction to the proposed marriage. Finally, after months of misery and reflection, Princess Margaret issued the following statement:

'I would like it to be known that I have decided not to marry Group Captain Townsend. I have been aware that, subject to my renouncing my rights of succession, it might have been possible for me to contract a civil marriage. But mindful of the Church's teaching that Christian marriage is indissoluble, and conscious of my duty to the Commonwealth, I have resolved to put these considerations before others.'

As the 1950s progressed, the Queen herself found the going increasingly rough. In the summer of 1957, John Grigg – then Lord Altrincham – fired a journalistic broadside against the Queen for her whole style, which he described as 'priggish schoolgirl surrounded by a conventional upper-class entourage'. He criticized her voice, and the press in general – in cartoons and comment – had a high old time. Traditionalists were sounding off cen-

However, 18 years later their separation proved that – in a society where divorce seems increasingly to be a part of marriage – royals, like commoners, can make unhappy decisions.

The sensational publicity which attended that tragic family episode – in the British as well as the foreign press – must have caused Queen Elizabeth great distress, even in a life familiar with gossip and criticism. She, like her predecessors this century, has even been accused of party political prejudice. Ironically, it was the Conservative Party – traditionally proud of its loyalty to the Crown – that involved her in this controversy. When Harold Macmillan left office in 1963, his successor had not been chosen. At that time, Conservative leaders 'emerged' from a process of wheeling and dealing within the upper 'magic circle' of the Party. The Queen, following her constitutional obligations, sought advice on how this process had gone and was told that Alec Douglas Home had the greatest support in the Party. His appointment astonished the country and angered many Tories outside the magic circle – and not a few within it. Some charged that the Queen had followed her personal inclinations in selecting this aristocrat to be Prime Minister. In fact, she had simply followed the advice of the outgoing Prime Minister – advice which he tendered for reasons best known to himself.

A more serious and more persistent cause of discontent among her subjects surrounds the matter of the Queen's income and accumulated assets. The few republicans in Parliament get little satisfaction when they press for details of the royal finances, and there are others – loyal monarchists – who are not entirely happy with the obscure system of taxed and untaxed revenues that combine to make the Queen of the United Kingdom one of the richest women in the world. Supporters estimate that at around £8,000,000 per annum (in 1976), the cost of the monarchy to the taxpayer is comparable to that of the average modern president, and is in any case fractionally cheaper than the annual Health Service bill for tranquilizers.

soriously against the critics; the critics were calling the Queen 'dowdy' and launching into her for appearing bored at official ceremonies which would have bored *them* stiff.

It is true that Elizabeth II is not particularly photogenic, which is a misfortune for probably the most photographed face in the world. It is also true that she is – as far as is possible for a person of her means, status and upbringing – ordinary and admirable in the way that the English approve. To put it kindly, there is nothing in her public life to suggest that she has a lively interest in the arts or music. In fact, we are told by her most recent biographer that her favourite television programmes are *Dad's Army* (a soap-opera) and *Kojak* (a cop show). Nevertheless, as everyone knows, she *is* a devotee of racing and an expert on the intricate lore of bloodstock. A lady who is, so to speak, happier at Newmarket races than in the royal box at Covent Garden, is not ill-fitted for the role of democratic monarch in modern Britain. It may irritate her intellectual subjects, but the rest are more at ease than they would be with an archaeologist on the throne. And, after all, Queen Elizabeth has produced an heir who plays the cello.

Even her devotion to family life strikes a responsive chord in 'post-permissive' Britain. The Royal family, despite – or possibly because of – its ups and downs, remains a model of domestic discipline and happiness that most of the Queen's subjects admire. When the film *Royal Family* appeared on the nation's television screens in 1969, it was an instant success. Shots of Prince Philip masterminding the family barbecue, the Queen in a village shop near Balmoral and Prince Charles playing his cello for an inquisitive younger brother all convinced her subjects – and millions of viewers throughout the world – that Queen Elizabeth, for all the 'stuffy' protocol that surrounds her, presides over a family not so different from many another.

Unfortunately, the parallels with modern family life do not stop there. In 1960, when Princess Margaret married the young photographer Antony Armstrong-Jones, Lord Snowdon, most people rejoiced with her in her happiness.

Left, Queen Elizabeth and Prince Philip seated in the Senate Chambers, Canberra, Australia. Above, the State Opening of Parliament, House of Lords in 1938.

That £8,000,000, of course, covers a host of official expenses that Parliament adjudges necessary for the functioning of the Head of State. However, even the Queen's annual 'personal allowance' of £980,000 had to cover many of the day-to-day running expenses that people in business would without hesitation charge to their companies. In addition, of course, the Queen also has her own enormous personal fortune from well-administered investments throughout the world. Because she is so public a person, many of her subjects feel she should be exposed to more public scrutiny in order to settle the vexed question of just how much wealth she controls, what she does with it, and who exactly spends it.

Despite the admiration of her people and the conscientious thoroughness with which she discharges her duties, Elizabeth II cannot hope to avoid being at the centre of controversy from time to time. For instance at the end of the 1950s, on the decision of her government, she played host to Chancellor Conrad Adenaue of West Germany. Even at that late date, and despite the fact that Germany was a cornerstone of the Western alliance, memories of the war caused some sectors of British public opinion to growl at this demonstration of friendship to the 'old enemy'. However, the Queen herself seemed to have enjoyed herself. As Prime Minister Macmillan recorded after a state dinner at Windsor Castle, at which Queen Juliana of the Netherlands was also a guest: 'The old Chancellor sat between the two Queens and flirted with both.' In the following year, 1959, the Queen returned the visit. Then she finally laid the ghost of Anglo–German rivalry, and the change of name forced on her family back in 1917, by going out of her way to draw attention to her German ancestry. In the 1970s, the monarch was again called upon to symbolize the mending of bridges with another former enemy,

when Emperor Hirohito of Japan was received on a State Visit. Predictably, the invitation was once again protested by war veterans.

It might be supposed that relations with members of the Commonwealth would pose few problems. However, on at least three occasions, the Commonwealth – which the Queen puts at the very top of her list of priorities – has presented problems calling forth

her large resources of courage and diplomatic insight. In November 1961, she was due to fly out on a State Visit to Ghana, which was then ruled by its mercurial dictator Dr Kwame Nkrumah. Britain viewed his regime as little better than a police state, and suspected that Nkrumah was being wooed by Russia. The Ghanaian leader seemed in the throes of heavy opposition, and parliamentarians at Westminster seriously questioned whether – with rumours rife of plots against the Ghanaian leader's life – the Queen herself would be safe. However, Elizabeth brushed all this aside with the common-sensical observation: 'How silly I should look if I was scared to visit Ghana and then Khruschchev went a few weeks later and had a good reception.' The visit went ahead and was a tumultuous success.

In 1964, the Queen's State Visit to Canada was a different matter altogether. Agitation for a French '*Quebec libre*' was at its height, and some French–Canadians viewed the forthcoming visit as a deliberate act of provo-

cation by the English–Canadians. There were rumours of planned assassination, and Elizabeth was indeed greeted with posters proclaiming 'Go Home'. In the event, the Queen fulfilled her schedule, but the visit was not a happy one.

At this time, however, more serious troubles were brewing elsewhere in the Commonwealth, as negotiations dragged on with the Rhodesian regime about transition to majority rule. Many Rhodesians, surprisingly ignorant of Britain's constitutional development over the past century, liked to suppose that Britain's resistance to their plans for continued white rule was due to an almost treacherous conspiracy by Harold Wilson's 'left-wing' government to prevent the Queen from following her own policy. Of course this was not only constitutional fantasy, but it was not even near to the Queen's own views on the situation. According to the Queen's approved biography, when Wilson flew to Salisbury, 'he carried a personal letter in the Queen's own handwriting'. This letter, apparently, made it crystal-clear to Smith that he was not a true servant of her and her Crown.

More recently, in the 1970s, many Australians were disgruntled with the Head of the Commonwealth when the High Commissioner – officially the Queen's representative in Australia, but in fact an appointee of the Australian government – dismissed the Prime Minister, Mr Gough Whitlam. Constitutionally, the power that made this possible derived from the prerogative of the Crown, but of course this manoeuvre in domestic Australian politics had nothing to do with Elizabeth, Queen of Australia, in person.

Whatever the occasional *contretemps* between her and her subjects, Elizabeth's Jubilee Celebrations of 1977 – to mark the 25th year of her accession – proved beyond any reasonable doubt that she still retains the personal love and respect of the overwhelming majority of the millions who acknowledge her as Queen and Head of the Commonwealth. In the United Kingdom itself, the celebrations evoked a surge of love and loyalty which surprised almost everyone – and irritated many commentators who would have preferred to see such a 'sentimental', even 'chauvinistic' occasion, treated with indifference. Instead, the British showed themselves proud of their monarch. The year before, Elizabeth had been an honoured guest at the celebrations of the 200th anniversary of the independence of the USA, which – in 1776 – overthrew the rule of her ancestor George III. Fortunately, the republican regime there is now well established, otherwise – from the warmth of her welcome wherever she went – one might have supposed that monarchism was on the way back.

Whatever lies ahead in the next 25 years of her reign, it seems unlikely that Elizabeth II will lose the affection and the admiration of the world.

Above left, *the Queen on 'walkabout' during her jubilee celebrations in 1977.* Above right, *the Queen and Prince Philip with Princess Anne and her husband Captain Mark Phillips, the young Prince Edward, Prince Andrew and Charles, Prince of Wales.* Left, *the royal silver wedding group, 1973.*

151

Where are they now?

✿✿✿✿✿✿✿✿✿✿✿✿✿✿✿✿✿✿✿✿✿✿✿✿✿✿✿✿✿✿✿

When King Paul and Queen Frederika of Greece were visiting the USA in 1958, their 18-year-old son, Crown Prince Constantine, met up with Simeon of Bulgaria, a few years his senior and student at Valley Forge Military Academy. Out for a drive, Prince Constantine at the wheel, they were flagged down for speeding. The cop began the routine of the note-book. 'What's your name?' he demanded of the driver. 'Crown Prince Constantine of Greece,' came the reply. 'Oh, yeah! And who's your friend?' 'Ex-King Simeon of Bulgaria,' came the reply. The station officer responded in kind with: 'And I'm J. Edgar Hoover.'

✿✿✿✿✿✿✿✿✿✿✿✿✿✿✿✿✿✿✿✿✿✿✿✿✿✿✿✿✿✿✿

To outsiders, the future of monarchy in the 20th century must seem uncertain. But kings and queens come of a tenacious breed. For instance, Constantine of Greece – given the history of his House – may still see reason to hope that one day he may return; while the Spanish monarchy has indeed been restored after more than four decades in exile. In fact, royal claims endure as long as there are members of the family prepared to advance the claim. Or, at least, that is how an uncompromising monarchist would see the case.

Of course, such hereditary principles no longer have any weight in the realm of practical politics. However, even in the constitutional theory of monarchies, mere precedence of birth has often not been sufficient to make a king or queen.

Simeon II, proud of his royal inheritance, remains one of a small, select band of ex-royals who have not given up all hope of once again leading their peoples. They consider it their duty to continue the traditions of their family. Another member of this band is His Imperial and Royal Highness Prince Louis Ferdinand of Hohenzollern, heir to the Crown of Prussia and the German Empire. Now in his early 70s, he lives in a stylish white residence, fittingly enough on the *Königsallee* ('King's Avenue') in the suburbs of Berlin – the city of his family for the past five centuries. As a young Prince, he was a familiar figure in America between the wars. He numbered among his friends Charlie Chaplin, Henry Ford and the air-ace, racing driver and airline executive Eddie Rickenbacker; and among his loves Lili Damita, a former wife of Errol Flynn. He has described his career with verve in the autobiographical *Rebel Prince*. Second son of the Kaiser's heir, ex-Crown Prince William, he found himself well and truly in the succession when, in 1933, his elder brother – also a William – renounced his dynastic rights so that he could contract a morganatic marriage.

In 1937, Prince Louis Ferdinand married Grand Duchess Kyra Kyrilovna of Russia. During the war he was an active member of the underground resistance to the Hitler regime. Afterwards, with the death of his father in 1951, the Prince became Head of the House of Hohenzollern, and took charge of the considerable family investments. The income from these investments is now used to pay appanages to members of the family and pensions to former retainers. The popularity of his aunt, the Princess Viktoria Luise, in her public appearances testifies to the nostalgia still felt for the old days of the monarchy in Germany. In reality, though, whether that nostalgia would ever lead to a restoration of the old regime is a somewhat fanciful question.

The case of Russia is, possibly, still more problematical. For there is among Europe's ex-royals a Pretender even to the throne of the Tsars. Born in 1917, His Imperial Highness the Grand Duke Vladimir Cyrilovitch, a second cousin of Nicholas II, is recognized as heir to the Crown of Imperial Russia. Before World War II he lived for a time in England, earning his living as a factory worker in Peterborough. As an incognito, he adopted the name Mikhailoff – as Peter the Great of Russia had done when he worked in British and Dutch shipyards. Nowadays, however, the Grand Duke lives in Madrid, where part of his income derives from the support of White Russian exiles. His daughter, the 26-year-old Grand Duchess Marie Vladimirovna, is his heiress to the title.

The realm of England is a classic example. Since Anglo–Saxon times the assent of the people has always, in theory at least, been necessary. In fact, at the coronation of William I, 'the Conqueror' in 1066, the people shouted their assent so vociferously that Norman soldiers guarding the approaches to Westminster Abbey dashed into the building, thinking there was a riot. When, in 1399, Henry IV forced the abdication of his cousin King Richard II, he was careful to have his claim confirmed by Parliament. Then, in 1485, Henry Tudor defeated and killed the last Plantagenet King, Richard III, at the Battle of Bosworth Field. Although his own relation to the royal line was remote – many Yorkist princes still living had a far better claim than he – Henry owed his Crown to conquest and the assent of Parliament.

In fact, the ultimate constitutional authority in England is 'the monarch in Parliament'. In 1701, the Act of Settlement established the succession to the Crown with the Electress Sophia of Hanover, grand-daughter of James I. Born in 1904, Prince Albert of Bavaria can also trace his descent from James I. It was his grandmother, Maria Theresa, who was acclaimed the rightful Queen of England – as 'Mary IV' – by the 'Assertion' nailed to the gates of St James's palace on the day of Victoria's death. Even today, there are some who consider Prince Albert the rightful monarch of England. However, the 1701 Act of Settlement will remain the sole legitimating principle of English monarchy unless it is changed by a future Act of the monarch in Parliament.

Monarchists also like to argue the rival 'legitimist' claims of at least two of the claimants to the 'Throne of France'. On the one hand, there is 71-year-old Monseigneur Henri d'Orleans, Count of Paris, who is descended from the Bourbons and actually takes his title of 'King Henry VI of France' seriously. On the other hand, supporters of 'His Imperial Highness, Prince Louis Napoleon Bonaparte' point to his descent from that 'Imperial' French dynasty inaugurated by the Corsican corporal who overthrew the revolutionary republican regime and crowned himself Emperor as Napoleon I in May 1804.

Both the Count of Paris – in the Foreign Legion – and Prince Louis Napoleon – a hero of the Resistance – fought loyally for their country during World War II. Both are good Frenchmen, but both cannot – even on the principles of royalist legitimacy – be considered 'rightful' King or Emperor. For their part, Bonapartists have to

assume that the Revolutionary overthrow of the Bourbon House in 1793 was a final and legitimate constitutional act. In contrast, Bourbonists have to accept that the 10th-century King, Hugh Capet, from whom all subsequent French Kings trace their descent, owed his Crown to an election by his fellow nobles. In fact, while crowns may be inherited, kingdoms have to start at some point in time before which the political community was ruled by some other institution from which that monarchy derived.

None of these theoretical considerations, however, prevent numerous monarchist organizations from claiming for their candidates the 'rightful' rule of those countries which have lost their monarchs during the 'democratic' years of the 20th century. These candidates are often people of real ability, who could undoubtedly distinguish themselves in the service of the state. They are excluded from such a role by their sincere attachment to their claim.

When Zog I and Queen Geraldine of Albania fled their country on 4 April 1939, for instance, they took with them the three-day-old Crown Prince Leka. The royal family lived near High Wycombe in England during the war, but the British would not help King Zog's return to Albania and he settled near Alexandria in Egypt. He died in France in 1961 at the age of 66. At a ceremony in the *Bristol Hotel* in Paris, a 'National Assembly' of Albanian exiles then acclaimed Leka the new King of the country.

In 1972, Leka presided over a 'Congress' of exiles in his home city of Madrid, and he remains convinced that there is still substantial monarchist feeling in communist Albania. His supporters boast that, as King Leka, he holds the allegiance of more Albanians (living outside the country) than the communist government controls within the borders of the country itself. It is certainly a fact that there are more than 80,000 Albanian exiles living in the USA alone, and the King keeps in close contact with the leaders of Albanian communities both there and elsewhere in the world. However, in early 1979, King Leka's activities were suddenly curtailed when the Spanish police

Above left, *ex-King Zog and Queen Geraldine of Albania, with four of the king's sisters.* Below left, *Queen Geraldine.* Left, *their son, Leka, aged 22, present claimant to the Albanian throne.* Right and previous page, *Constantine of the Hellenes.*

raided his home and found a large quantity of arms and ammunition there. Although the King protested that his armoury was purely for his own use, the Spanish government nonetheless asked him to leave the country. As a result, the King of Albania is now to be found in Rhodesia – still, no doubt, in close contact with his supporters around the world.

In complete contrast, the heir to the Yugoslav Crown has stubbornly refused to activate his claim. When the former Crown Prince, Alexander, was born in London in 1945, it was already clear that his father, King Peter II, would not regain his throne. Depressed at what he saw as betrayal by Britain and America, the young monarch also found himself running into financial difficulties. As a result, the family had to abandon their expensive suite in *Claridge's Hotel* and move to the London Yugoslav embassy-in-exile. Later, they lived in France and America, where the King worked for a while as a consultant on international affairs. However, his attempts to recoup his fortunes by financial speculation soon brought worse problems in their train. Increasingly he turned to alcohol and in 1970, at the age of 47, he died – almost destitute – in California. His son Alexander's decision not to pursue his claims as King has, predictably, caused consternation among keen monarchists.

Tsar Simeon II of Bulgaria, on the other hand, takes a quite different view of his position. In 1969, he announced to the world: 'We Bulgars look confidently to the future, convinced that freedom, justice and welfare will finally triumph in our land.' Undoubtedly this is the ultimate goal in life for him who is still 'King of the Bulgars', and whose thoughts are turned constantly towards Bulgaria.

Born in 1937, the second child and only son of Tsar Boris III, Simeon began his reign in 1943 under a Council of Regents. The next year, Russia declared war and entered Bulgaria. The opposition forces in the country – the Communist Party, Agrarian Party and pro-Russian army elements – then seized power. A brief period of coalition government followed, but this was terminated by a Communist takeover. Finally, in 1945, Simeon's uncle Prince Kyril and 225 others of the regency regime were executed. In September the following year, the Communist Party stage-managed a referendum which purported to show a large majority against the monarchy. At this point the nine-year-old King went into exile in Egypt with his mother and sister. He was educated at Victoria College in Alexandria and the Lycée Français in Madrid before leaving Europe for the USA. There he entered the Valley Forge Military Academy in Wayne, Pennsylvania. He registered as Mr Rylski, Cadet No. 6883, and graduated in 1959. Nowadays he lives in Madrid and Switzerland, and describes himself as: 'A jack of all trades, primarily in-terested in business, banking and politics – some call it "statesmanship".'

In 1962, Simeon married Dona Margarita Gomez-Aceboy Cojuela, the daughter of a former Spanish marquis. They have four sons and a daughter. The eldest child, 17-year-old Prince Kardam, is now Simeon's heir. Meanwhile, the Tsar and his Chancellery, based in Madrid, keep up active contacts with exiles around the world, but Simeon also believes that Bulgaria still has many pro-monarchist enthusiasts. In this he may be right, since in September 1974 a Bulgarian court convicted one Boris Arsov Iliev for 'counter-revolutionary acts', describing him as 'an inveterate monarchist'.

Another deposed monarch from the same part of Europe who also maintains his claim is 58-year-old King Michael of Romania. However, he also has a busy career which has included a representation for the Lockheed Aircraft Corporation. For him, hopes of restoration can only be a dream. Although the celebration of his 24th birthday in November 1945 brought over 50,000 people onto the streets of Bucharest to demonstrate their loyalty, Michael was nonetheless forced into exile in December 1947. He is now married to Anne of Bourbon Parma, and the bitterness of exile is largely forgotten by this successful businessman and father of five daughters.

The seeming stability of the communist regime now ruling the Balkan countries is in sharp contrast to the turbulent state of Italy, across the Adriatic Sea. A

candidate for the succession than the Prince of Naples himself.

Nowadays, in the unsettled state of Italian politics, such concern over the succession is not necessarily absurd. Indeed, monarchists' hopes fluttered elsewhere in the Latin world with the death of the Portuguese dictator Salazar in 1974. Then, HRH Dom Duarte Nuno, Duke of Braganza – 'a small, bothered man, completely lost in an enormous palace (in Coimbra)' – the claimant to the Portuguese throne, thought for some months that perhaps his country might recall him. However, as he enters his 70s, it must be clear to him that his hopes were groundless. After his death, his title will pass to his son and heir, Dom Duarte Pio – who is in his mid-30s. Whether his future holds a crown is a question for him and the Portuguese. It is also the kind of question that has exercised people in many other monarchist circles. For, with all the colour and heroism of its past, it seems that the 'Age of Monarchy' is approaching its final chapter in many of the countries surveyed in this book.

Far left, *Princess Maria Pia of Italy and Alexander of Yugoslavia*. Above left, *Prince Vittorio Emanuele of Italy and his sister Princess Maria Gabriella*. Bottom left, *Tsar Simeon II of the Bulgarians with his fiancée, Margarita Gómez-Acebo y Cejuela, in August 1961*. Below, *Prince (later King) Michael with his father, King Carol II of Romania, in London, November 1938*.

cynic might say that the situation there could be no worse even under a monarchy. King Umberto II certainly believes it could be much better and, though in his 70s, he would dearly like the job. In 1944, his father – Victor Emmanuel III – delegated the royal power to him as Regent; in May the old King abdicated. In a plebiscite 55% of the voters declared for a republic, and Umberto – King for just a month – went into exile. But he did not abdicate.

His father died in exile in Egypt in 1947, and Umberto now lives in Portugal. Although he has been closely involved with Italy's major monarchist organization, the *Unione Monarchica Italiana*, he does not approve of the small Italian monarchist political parties even though they have had – on occasion – as many as nine seats in the country's legislature. The ageing monarch and his entourage have often been compared to a court-in-exile, but the future of the dynasty is uncertain. His four children by his wife Princess Marie Rose – from whom he has been separated for over 20 years – have all lived life to the full and ignored the kind of inhibitions normally associated with royalty. The escapades of his youngest daughter have made headlines; his eldest daughter has been divorced; while his heir, Crown Prince Victor Emmanuel, now 42, caused scandal

amongst monarchists by his long-established liaison with a commoner, Marina Doria, whom he then married in Las Vegas. Although King Umberto has recognized his son's wife as 'Her Royal Highness the Princess of Naples', many old-fashioned monarchists feel that the King's nephew – HRH Amedeo, Duke of Aosta – would make a more suitable

Index

Acknowledgements

The publishers would like to thank the following for their kind permission to reproduce the photographs in this book:

Clive Bubley: 9; Camera Press: 1, 8–9, 51 below left and right, 86, 87, 91 below, 107, 117 below, 126 above, 127 below, 148 below, 148–9, 150 above, 150–1 below, 152–3; The Cooper Bridgeman Library Ltd: 26–7, 34–5, 133 above; Anwar Hussein: 151; John Frost Newspaper Collection: 63; John Topham Picture Library: 46 above; Mary Evans Picture Library: 2–3, 12, 16–17, 18–19, 19, 20, 21–2, 24 above and below, 28 above and below, 30–1, 34, 35, 42, 54–6, 65 above right, 72–3, 74 below left, 75 above right, 76–7, 88, 90 above and centre, 92–3, 94 left, 101 right, 112 above, 128–30 above left, 134 above left, 134–5 above; The National Railway Museum: 10 above left, 11 above right; Popperfoto: 29–30, 32 above and below, 33 above and below, 39, 40 above, 41 below and below, 42 (inset), 43, 44 above and below, 45, 46 below, 47, 51 above, 53 left and right, 58, 59, 61, 62–3, 66–7, 68 above, 69, 70 above and below, 72–3 below, 79, 84, 85, 91 above and centre, 98–9, 99, 100 above right, 101 left, 102–5, 106–7 above, 108–9 below, 110 above left and below, 114–16 above left, 117 above, 120, 124 above and centre, 125, 127 above, 135 below right, 136, 143 below, 154–7 above: Radio Times Hulton Picture Library: 10–11, 12–13, 14 below left and right, 14–15, 18, 22–3, 23, 24–5, 25, 36, 36–7, 38–9, 40 below, 48–9, 50, 52, 57, 58–9, 60–1, 64 above left, centre and below left, 64–5, 66, 67 below, 68 below, 71, 72 above left, 74–5 above, 75 below right, 78–9, 80–1, 81, 82 left and right, 83 above and below, 93, 94–5, 95, 96–7 above, 97 below, 106 below, 108 above left, 108–9 above, 110–111, 111, 112–13 below, 113 above and below, 116 above right, 116–17, 118–19, 119, 121, 122 left, 122–3 above, 123 below, 124 below, 126 below, 130–1 below, 132 above left, 134–5 below, 137 above, 138 above and below, 142–3 above, 157 below; Spectrum Colour Library: 17, 100 above left; Wartski, London: 49; Zefa Picture Library: 4–7, 73 above, 78–9, 88–9.

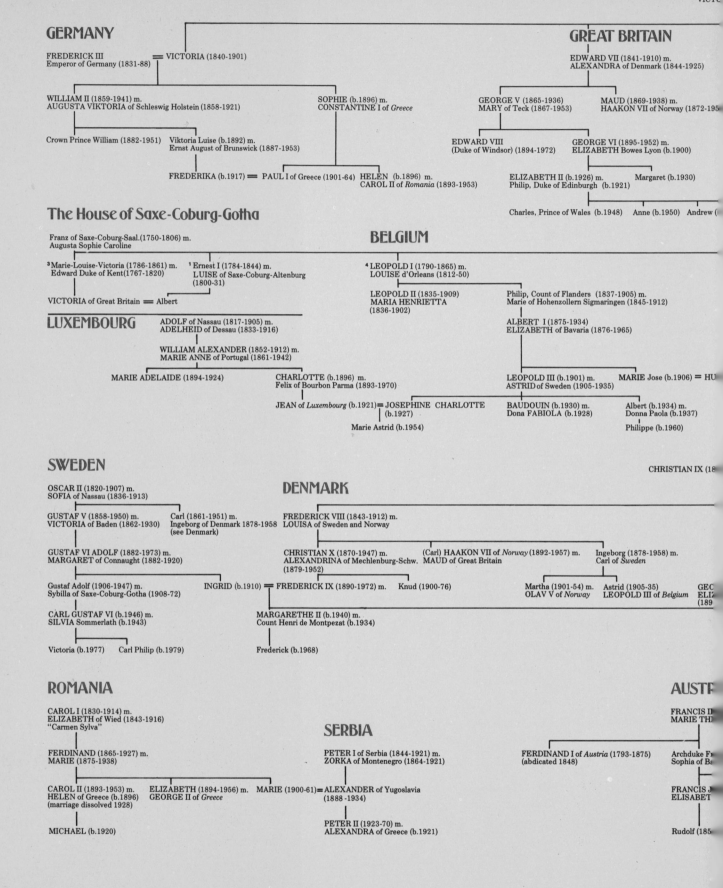

GERMANY

FREDERICK III
Emperor of Germany (1831-88) ══ VICTORIA (1840-1901)

WILLIAM II (1859-1941) m.
AUGUSTA VIKTORIA of Schleswig Holstein (1858-1921)

SOPHIE (b.1896) m.
CONSTANTINE I of *Greece*

Crown Prince William (1882-1951)   Viktoria Luise (b.1892) m.
Ernst August of Brunswick (1887-1953)

FREDERIKA (b.1917) ══ PAUL I of Greece (1901-64)   HELEN (b.1896) m.
CAROL II of *Romania* (1893-1953)

GREAT BRITAIN

EDWARD VII (1841-1910) m.
ALEXANDRA of Denmark (1844-1925)

GEORGE V (1865-1936)   MAUD (1869-1938) m.
MARY of Teck (1867-1953)   HAAKON VII of Norway (1872-195

EDWARD VIII
(Duke of Windsor) (1894-1972)   GEORGE VI (1895-1952) m.
ELIZABETH Bowes Lyon (b.1900)

ELIZABETH II (b.1926) m.   Margaret (b.1930)
Philip, Duke of Edinburgh (b.1921)

Charles, Prince of Wales (b.1948)   Anne (b.1950)   Andrew (

The House of Saxe-Coburg-Gotha

Franz of Saxe-Coburg-Saal.(1750-1806) m.
Augusta Sophie Caroline

³ Marie-Louise-Victoria (1786-1861) m.   ¹ Ernest I (1784-1844) m.
Edward Duke of Kent(1767-1820)   LUISE of Saxe-Coburg-Altenburg
(1800-31)

VICTORIA of Great Britain ══ Albert

LUXEMBOURG

ADOLF of Nassau (1817-1905) m.
ADELHEID of Dessau (1833-1916)

WILLIAM ALEXANDER (1852-1912) m.
MARIE ANNE of Portugal (1861-1942)

MARIE ADELAIDE (1894-1924)   CHARLOTTE (b.1896) m.
Felix of Bourbon Parma (1893-1970)

JEAN of *Luxembourg* (b.1921) ══ JOSEPHINE CHARLOTTE
(b.1927)

Marie Astrid (b.1954)

BELGIUM

⁴ LEOPOLD I (1790-1865) m.
LOUISE d'Orleans (1812-50)

LEOPOLD II (1835-1909)   Philip, Count of Flanders (1837-1905) m.
MARIA HENRIETTA   Marie of Hohenzollern Sigmaringen (1845-1912)
(1836-1902)

ALBERT I (1875-1934)
ELIZABETH of Bavaria (1876-1965)

LEOPOLD III (b.1901) m.   MARIE Jose (b.1906) ══ HU
ASTRID of Sweden (1905-1935)

BAUDOUIN (b.1930) m.   Albert (b.1934) m.
Dona FABIOLA (b.1928)   Donna Paola (b.1937)

Philippe (b.1960)

CHRISTIAN IX (18

SWEDEN

OSCAR II (1820-1907) m.
SOFIA of Nassau (1836-1913)

GUSTAF V (1858-1950) m.   Carl (1861-1951) m.
VICTORIA of Baden (1862-1930)   Ingeborg of Denmark 1878-1958
(see Denmark)

GUSTAF VI ADOLF (1882-1973) m.
MARGARET of Connaught (1882-1920)

Gustaf Adolf (1906-1947) m.   INGRID (b.1910) ══ FREDERICK IX (1890-1972)
Sybilla of Saxe-Coburg-Gotha (1908-72)

CARL GUSTAF VI (b.1946) m.
SILVIA Sommerlath (b.1943)

Victoria (b.1977)   Carl Philip (b.1979)

DENMARK

FREDERICK VIII (1843-1912) m.
LOUISA of Sweden and Norway

CHRISTIAN X (1870-1947) m.   (Carl) HAAKON VII of *Norway* (1892-1957) m.   Ingeborg (1878-1958) m.
ALEXANDRINA of Mechlenburg-Schw.   MAUD of Great Britain   Carl of *Sweden*
(1879-1952)

Martha (1901-54) m.   Astrid (1905-35)   GEO
OLAV V of *Norway*   LEOPOLD III of *Belgium*   ELIZ
(189

FREDERICK IX (1890-1972)   Knud (1900-76)

MARGARETHE II (b.1940) m.
Count Henri de Montpezat (b.1934)

Frederick (b.1968)

ROMANIA

CAROL I (1830-1914) m.
ELIZABETH of Wied (1843-1916)
"Carmen Sylva"

FERDINAND (1865-1927) m.
MARIE (1875-1938)

CAROL II (1893-1953) m.   ELIZABETH (1894-1956) m.   MARIE (1900-61) ══ ALEXANDER of Yugoslavia
HELEN of Greece (b.1896)   GEORGE II of *Greece*   (1888 -1934)
(marriage dissolved 1928)

MICHAEL (b.1920)

SERBIA

PETER I of Serbia (1844-1921) m.
ZORKA of Montenegro (1864-1921)

PETER II (1923-70) m.
ALEXANDRA of Greece (b.1921)

AUSTR

FRANCIS I
MARIE THI

FERDINAND I of *Austria* (1793-1875)   Archduke Fi
(abdicated 1848)   Sophia of Ba

FRANCIS J
ELISABET

Rudolf (185